St. Michael's Episcopal Church

The 125th Year of Its Founding

ANTHONY M. SAMMARCO

America Through Time®
ADDING COLOR TO AMERICAN HISTORY

10877985

This book is dedicated to the Glory of God
and to St. Michael the Archangel

America Through Time is an imprint of Fonthill Media LLC
www.through-time.com
office@through-time.com

Published by Arcadia Publishing by arrangement with Fonthill Media LLC
For all general information, please contact Arcadia Publishing:
Telephone: 843-853-2070
Fax: 843-853-0044
E-mail: sales@arcadiapublishing.com
For customer service and orders:
Toll-Free 1-888-313-2665

www.arcadiapublishing.com

First published 2023

Copyright © St. Michael's Episcopal Church 2023

ISBN 978-1-63499-434-7

All rights reserved. No part of this publication may be reproduced, stored in a retrieval system or transmitted in any form or by any means, electronic, mechanical, photocopying, recording or otherwise, without prior permission in writing from Fonthill Media LLC

Typeset in Mrs Eaves XL Serif Narrow
Printed and bound in England

Contents

Acknowledgments

I wish to especially thank the Adult Education Commission at St. Michael's Church for the support and direction of this book: Lana Agnew, Stacey Brown, Martha Cotton, Sargon Donabed, Bob Hamblet, Bob Hiss, Jesse Hughes, Carolyn Lyons, Sheila Monks, Heather Putnam and Angela McConney Scheepers.

I wish to extend my sincere thanks and deep appreciation to: The Rev. Hall Kirkham, Rector; The Rev. Jennifer Daly, Associate Deacon; Leo Biocchi, Minister of Families & Communications Director; Nanette Diaute, Office Administrator; Dennis Mackler, Sexton.

The Wardens and Vestry of St. Michael's Church: Bob Hiss, Senior Warden; Kate Hamblet, Junior Warden; Lorna Martin, Clerk; Scott Stikeleather, Treasurer. Members of the Vestry: Dina Bray; John Duff; Carolyn Lyons; Nate O'Connell; Ama Okey-Igwe; Candace Paris; Andrew Synnott; Alex Whiteside; Susie Swanson; Ron Iacobucci; Derek Schoettle; Heather Putnam. Delegates to the Diocesan Convention: Dina Bray and Scott Bell. Representatives to the Neponset River Deanery: Steven Wilson and Becky Simonds. Trustees of Garden of Seasons: Ingrid Beattie, Robin Putnam and Cat Rogerson.

I would also like to extend my thanks to: Bess Allen; Jim Anderson; Archives of American Art, Smithsonian Institution; Bob and Betty Applegate; Kai Bridge Armstrong; Frank J. Van Atta; Anne Aylward; Todd Beckham; Robert Bernheim; Margery M. Buckingham; Dr. Richard R. Bunbury; Brink Bush; Reverend Joyce Caggiano; Cesidio "Joe" Cedrone; Marilyn Cheney; The Charles J. Connick Stained Glass Foundation; Ann Clifford; Edie Clifford; Reverend Ellis Clifton; George Corbett; Cram and Ferguson LLC, Ethan Anthony, AIA ICTP; Digital Commonwealth; Lisa Elliot; Forest Hills Cemetery, Janis Stetz; Roger Sherman Greene; Harvard Library; the late Kay Herzog; Ryan Heyward; Patricia A. Hogan; George Kalchev, Fonthill Media; Library of Congress; Reverend Victor Kazanjian; Peter Bryant Kingman; Kena Longabaugh Smith; Joe McKendry; Reverend Jennifer McCracken; Reverend Karen Maleri; Massachusetts Charitable Mechanics Association; Milton Cemetery, Lisa Ahearn; Milton Library, Jean Hlady, Head of Adult Services/Reference; *Milton Times*, Patricia Desmond, Publisher; Beth Neville; Organ Historical Society; Reverend Sherry Osborn; Barratt Park; Linda Mason Pirie; James R. Stettner; Orleans Camera; Reverend Eleanor Ross Jones Panasevich; Lilian M.C. Randall; Lynn Bernheim Reese; Ellie Wendell Reiter; Chris Rinderer; The Right Reverend Samuel Sewell Rodman III; Vicki Rugo; St. Alban's Episcopal Church, Syracuse,

New York, Rev. Julie Calhoun-Bryant; St. Paul's School, Baltimore; Ron Scully; Antony Shearn; Dennis Sheehan; Brian A. Sullivan; Alan Sutton, Fonthill Media; Jamie Sutton; Charles and Mary Byers Truslow; the Virginia Episcopal School; John P. Whiteside.

I want to especially thank Sheila Monks for her invaluable assistance in her proofreading and editing of this book.

All photographs are from the Archives of St. Michael's Church unless otherwise noted.

He who led God's armies against Satan's forces in the Book of Revelation, where during the war in heaven he defeats Satan.

A detail of the Reynolds Memorial Window depicting St. Michael the Archangel who is regarded as guardian of the Church and its members against the evil one. It is he who is supposed to weigh the souls of humanity on the Last Day, and the scales are seen depicted at the top of the window. (Photo by Peter B. Kingman)

INTRODUCTION

A Prayer to St. Michael the Archangel from the novel *Ulysses* by James Joyce:

Blessed Michael, the archangel, defend us in the hour of conflict.
Be our safeguard against the wickedness and snares of the devil
may God restrain him, we humbly pray:
and do thou, O Prince of the heavenly host,
by the power of God thrust Satan down to hell
and with him those other wicked spirits
who wander through the world for the ruin of souls.

Amen.

It was in 1895 that a group of Milton residents including the Gannett, Herrick, Hollis, Jackson, Lee, Reynolds, Richardson, Stevens, Whitney and Wilde families, led by Ellen Maria Wilde, requested from Bishop William Lawrence that Episcopal services be held at Fraternity Hall, the third-floor assembly hall in the Associates Building on Adams Street in Milton Village. Previously, those in Milton seeking to attend Episcopal worship might go to St. Mary's Church at Upham's Corner or All Saints Church at Ashmont in Dorchester, the Church of the Holy Spirit in Mattapan or Christ Church in Quincy. From that time until 1898, the Episcopal Mission in Milton served the needs of the Episcopal community.

In the *Milton News* on October 5, 1895 Bishop Lawrence wrote a letter to the new Episcopal congregation in Milton. An extract of that letter stated: "As our suburban communities grow and the houses begin to thicken it is well that the church should enter upon her work early and thus gain the affections and confidence not only of those who would naturally come to her, but those who without her might drift away from all institutional religious life. Our church by the beauty of her ritual, the dignity of her worship, the simplicity of her creed, by her breadth of charity, and practical spirit does appeal to many people who have not been brought up in her fold. Our church enters a town not to weaken other Christian bodies but to do her part in the strengthening of the spiritual life of the community."

With the laying of the granite cornerstone bearing the signs of the Alpha and the Omega in 1898, the simple but impressive design of the new church was that of William Ralph

Emerson, a well-respected architect who was long recognized as being influential in the development of late nineteenth-century architecture. Bishop Lawrence said when the cornerstone was laid, "St. Michael's comes to the town [of Milton] in no spirit of rivalry, but as one added factor in the uplifting of the spiritual life of the community." Emerson lived across the street from the church. His son, Ralph Lincoln Emerson, a promising and gifted architect who worked in his father's architectural office as a draftsman at this time, is said to have assisted in the design of the Rectory. He was a friend of Ralph Adams Cram, a draftsman in the architectural firm of Rotch & Tilden in Boston just after his graduation from Harvard in 1891. Interestingly, Arthur Rotch designed the Church of the Holy Spirit in Mattapan and Cram the Parish Hall. Cram would also design the Parish House that was built adjacent to St. Michael's Church in 1911.

St. Michael's Church was built in 1898 in the "early English style of architecture" of rough coursed blocks of seam-faced granite. John Alden Lee said of the design "I can judge it is going to make a very cozy little structure." Built in what was said by the *Church Militant* as "one of the most beautiful suburbs of Boston" on Randolph Avenue within an impressive residential area, the church was set on a portion of the George R.R. Rivers estate, formerly that of Governor Thomas Hutchinson, that extended from Adams Street to Randolph Avenue. The church was the first Episcopal church in Milton, and its design and setting emulated that of an English village church. In fact, the *Milton Record* on December 1, 1917 stated "Mr. Emerson was one of the first [architects] to break away from the ungainly styles of the middle of the past century, and to insist that a [design] should combine artistic merit with utility."

In the *Church Militant* in October 1898 Reverend Theodore Irving Reese said: "St. Michael's Church, Milton, is the answer to the needs of the people. It came by invitation." Reese was highly regarded at the Episcopal Theological School and Bishop Lawrence said of him: "Some men's characters are so normal, simple and true that they can best be interpreted, not by adjectives and explanations, but by the facts and the course of their lives. Such a man was Theodore Irving Reese."

St. Michael's Church, as originally designed, consisted of a nave and small chancel, with seating for two hundred. The church was built for a congregation in a suburban town, and the parish consisted of a "community of well-to-do people," many of whom kept houses in Boston. The church was a credit to Emerson as "with his artistic ability he possessed great ingenuity and a quickness in perceiving possibilities in seemingly unpromising material." With its asymmetrical stone tower that also served as the lancet-arched entrance, it was in 1904 to receive a piece of stone from the Milton Abbey in Milton Abbas, Dorset, England. At the request of Reverend Reese, a piece of the ancient Norman abbey was sent to Milton by Sir Everard Alexander Hambro, the Lord of the Manor of Milton Abbas. It was incorporated as a keystone over the inner entrance of St. Michael's Church and served as an important link to connect the two churches. Interestingly, St. Michael was a patron saint of Milton Abbey since the time of King Athelstan, King of the Anglo-Saxons from 924 to 927 and King of the English from 927 until his death in 939.

As the parish increased in size, a Tudor Revival half-timbered Parish House, with stucco emulating medieval wattle and daub, was built in 1911. With a growing congregation, the chancel of the church was enlarged in 1916 with an impressive stained-glass window designed by Ralph Adams Cram that was placed above the altar, which was designed by John Evans. The Rectory of St. Michael's Church, which was built in 1898, was also designed by Emerson, assisted by his son Ralph Lincoln Emerson. A substantial asymmetrical Shingle-style house with a sloping shed-like dormered roof in the distinctive style of William Ralph Emerson, the rectory was originally built closer to the church, on the present site of the driveway, and was moved to its present location in 1953.

Since its founding, St. Michael's Church has warmly welcomed all who wish to join in worship and fully supports each person's unique and individual spiritual journey. A closely knit community of faith and prayer has empowered the congregation to be the manifestation of Christ's love in the world. Grounded in the rich tradition of Anglican liturgy, the congregation is also open to creative expressions of worship as a path toward holiness and spiritual growth. St. Michael's continues to actively encourage full participation in all areas of worship, outreach and other aspects of its busy parish life.

The many opportunities for lay leadership challenge and inspire parishioners to enter into multiple ministries, as they personally contribute their passions and talents while discovering new skills and spiritual gifts. Such opportunities include lay preaching, educational offerings, wide-ranging outreach programs, adult and youth choirs, and a vibrant church school. It is by the congregation's caring support for each other, and its dedication to enriching the life of the parish through participation in its many ministries, that the strong bond of St. Michael's community is formed and continually renewed.

It is this sense of a supportive and accepting community, identified by an overwhelming majority of parishioners as the most important quality of St. Michael's Church, that brings this diverse group of Christians of all ages together, week after week, to worship, pray, sing, learn, enjoy fellowship and minister to each other and the world beyond our doors.

This pencil sketch of the proposed St. Michael's Episcopal Church was drawn by William Ralph Emerson in 1897. The church was of an "early English style of architecture," built of rough coursed granite blocks set in a random ashlar design with a crenelated battlement tower.

125 YEARS
Fulfilling Our Future

St. Michael's Episcopal Church
EST. 1895

It sounds self-serving and predictable that the Rector of a parish church would laud that parish and its church as special, especially in a book produced in recognition of that parish church's 125th anniversary. So let me share what many at St. Michael's have already heard; that at the time I was in my third year of seminary I was invited to do my field education there, and my wife Marjorie, who is deeply reflective and, to be delicate, was at the time relatively 'reserved' as a person of faith, confided that, "if you could serve a place like St. Michael's, I'd come to church." Admittedly more committed in my faith than she, I still knew precisely what she meant.

"It's a very special place," Sam Rodman, the former Rector and my field education supervisor, told me when I remarked how welcome and validated, I felt as seminarian here. Meeting Bob Appleyard, Sam's predecessor, whose name is spoken with great affection in the church halls, for the first time I was struck by his show of vulnerability at my news of the parish: his glistening eyes, and his soft smile the kind of smile, that one deeply loving of another shows when hearing about their lives. A church building can offer space set apart that allows prayer and silent contemplation, life, ministry and fellowship, and St. Michael's has provided that for any who come. The people who gather in worship and share the bread of thanksgiving, who gather to share their journey towards recovery or to support those whose loved ones are suffering, who gather to bless newborns, bring loving couples together, and bury family members- all of them release their considerable prayers to these very wooden rafters, which receive and absorb them, resonating the yearning for God that I believe we all carry.

Church is only partly a building. It is more I think the gathered community sharing the mysteries of life's themes and an invitation to find purpose and meaning in life by building a relationship with God. St. Michael's Church is guided by the life and teachings of Jesus Christ, which in scripture we hear, read, mark, learn and inwardly digest, and which we experience through the presence and power of one another and the Holy Spirit, all in the pursuit of God's mission towards doing justice, practicing compassion, and seeking the reconciliation of a torn and broken world.

St. Michael's does that, I recognized early on, in a way that feels distinctive: parishioners are its personality" or maybe "its essence". St. Michael's Church is deeply expresses of this particular household of God gathered on Randolph Avenue in Milton, Massachusetts, at work in the community and the world. In this book, you will learn about them, about how this all came to be, and maybe something about how God is inviting this parish church, and you, to help build the realm God envisions for God's Creation.

Please come to our door and we will greet you warmly into a place where our paths towards relationship with God can come together. St. Michael's has met me at the place where I am learning about what a parish church is and can be, opening its door onto that possibility.

In peace, and with deep and abiding gratitude,

The Rev. Hall Kirkham
Milton, Massachusetts

112 Randolph Avenue, Milton, MA 02186
p: 617.698.1813 f: 617.698.3437 e: mail@stmichaelsmilton.org
www.stmichaelsmilton.org

1

St. Michael the Archangel

Yet Michael the archangel, when contending with the devil he disputed about the body of Moses, durst not bring against him a railing accusation, but said, The Lord rebuke thee.

Jude 1:9

The Three Archangels with Tobias was painted c. 1467 by Francesco Botticini. He is seen with the archangels Michael, Gabriel, and Raphael who are named in Scripture, and who played important roles in the history of salvation. St. Michael the Archangel is the "Prince of the Heavenly Host," the leader of all angels. In Hebrew, his name means "who is like God," which was the battle cry of the angels against Lucifer and his followers after they rebelled against God. Seen with St. Gabriel, whose name means "God's strength," and St. Raphael whose name means "God has healed." Tobias, seen in the center, was the only child of a blind holy man named Tobit and his wife Anna, who were Jews from Nineveh circa 700 BC. Tobit sent his young son Tobias on an errand to a distant land to collect monies that were owed to him. (Uffizi Gallery, Florence)

St. Michael Weighing Souls During the Last Judgement was painted in the fifteenth century and used to illustrate Antiphonale Cisterciense. This is a detail of a much larger illuminated manuscript that depicts St. Michael holding the scales to weigh souls. In his other hand is his sword. According to the renowned historian Lilian M. C. Randall, "This fine antiphonary illustration is reminiscent of illustrations in the deluxe King Wenceslas Bible, Czech, late 14th-century." (Collection Rein Abbey, Austria)

There was silence in heaven
When the dragon fought with the Archangel Michael.
The voice of a thousand was heard saying:
Salvation, honour and power be to almighty God.

Lesson I from the Prophet Daniel

St. Michael was painted by Piero della Francesca, a noted fifteenth-century Italian painter, who by 1439 was working in Florence with Domenico Veneziano, whose treatment of space must have influenced him. Francesca depicted the saint in a natural, almost realistic pose. The four aspects of St. Michael are: to fight against Satan; to rescue the souls of the faithful from the power of the enemy, especially at the hour of death; to be the champion of God's people; to call away from earth and bring men's souls to judgment. (Collection of National Gallery, London)

St. Michael Fighting the Dragon is from the Book of Hours of Étienne Chevalier, illuminated by Jean Fouquet who was an illuminator from Tours in the fifteenth century. (Collection Upton House, Lord Bearsted Collection, London)

> Then war broke out in heaven; Michael and his angels battled against the dragon. The dragon and its angels fought back, but they did not prevail and there was no longer any place for them in heaven. The huge dragon, the ancient serpent, who is called the Devil and Satan, who deceived the whole world, was thrown down to earth, and its angels were thrown down with it.
>
> Revelation 12:7-9

Archangel Michael Hurls the Rebellious Angels into the Abyss, c. 1666 was painted by Luca Giordano (1632–1705). This dramatic and highly charged painting depicts the struggling St. Michael, who visually symbolized the triumph of light over the rebellion of the powers of darkness, with his foot on a writhing Lucifer surrounded by the denizens of Hell. Archangel Michael is the commander of angelic armies and takes this responsibility quite seriously. (Collection of Kunsthistorisches Museum, Vienna)

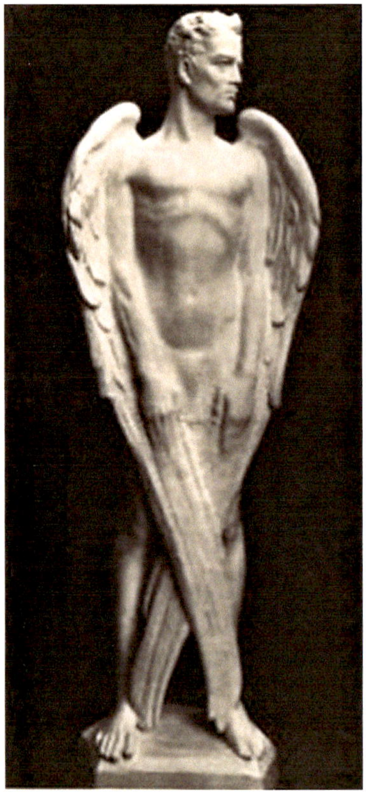

Above left: St. Michael was painted by Guido Reni in 1636. The painting hangs in Santa Maria della Concezione Church, Rome. St. Michael dramatically stands as the Prince of the Heavenly Hosts, guarding the world by his sword over those residents who seem determined to dethrone and replace God. (Santa Maria della Concezione, Rome)

> And there was war in heaven: Michael and his angels fought against the dragon; and the dragon fought and his angels, and prevailed not; neither was their place found any more in heaven. And the great dragon was cast out, that old serpent, called the Devil, and Satan, which deceiveth the whole world: he was cast out into the earth, and his angels were cast out with him.
>
> Revelation 12: 7-9

Above right: This photograph is of *The Aviator*, a statue of St. Michael that was done by Anna Coleman Watts Ladd (1878–1939), a noted sculptress and founding member of the Guild of Boston Artists, who kept a weekend house in Milton. Though known for her sculptures, she was recognized for her work in creating prosthetics for disfigured World War I soldiers from extremely thin galvanized copper. The metal facemasks were painted with hard enamel to resemble the recipient's skin tone, with real hair to create the eyelashes, eyebrows and mustaches. It was to be her great claim to fame that in 1932, the French Government honored her as a Chevalier de la Légion d'Honneur, in recognition of the work she'd done. This photograph hangs in the Lower Parish Hall, and was given in memory of John Franklin Crocker III and Thomas Roberts Shewell, two Milton Academy students who drowned in 1932 while canoeing on Cape Cod.

2

Beginnings of St. Michael's Episcopal Church

The Lord hath done great things for us, whereof we are glad.

Psalm cxxvi. 3

This ink drawing of St. Michael's Church was done by William Ralph Emerson and more closely resembles the church as it was eventually built in 1899. Though it was considered a small church, seating only two hundred worshippers, it was an impressive design by a renowned architect with a prominent asymmetrical crenelated battlement tower with a curious cock vane surmounting its low-pitched roof.

For we are labourers together with God: ye are God's husbandry, ye are God's building.

1 Corinthians 3:9

The Associates Hall Building in Milton Village was built in 1882 and designed by Arthur Rotch and George Thomas Tilden, partners in Rotch and Tilden, who were considered the "Society Architects" of late nineteenth-century Boston. Rotch was graduated from Harvard and both men attended the Massachusetts Institute of Technology and the École des Beaux-Arts in Paris, and had apprenticed at the architectural firm of Ware and Brunt. Seen here, the ground floor had the William H. Puffer Pharmacy (later the Milton Hill Pharmacy), a branch of the Milton Library, and other stores. On the third floor was Fraternity Hall which, according to Bishop Lawrence, was accessed by "two flights of stairs [which] were not too much for faithful Episcopalians to mount for their worship." (Author's collection)

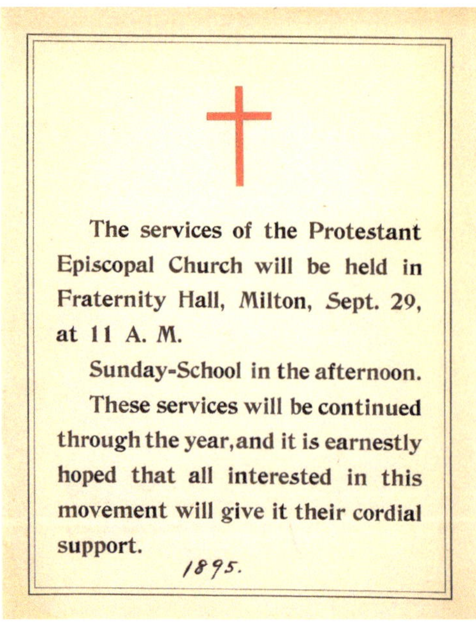

The services of the Protestant Episcopal Church will be held in Fraternity Hall, Milton, Sept. 29, at 11 A. M.

Sunday-School in the afternoon.

These services will be continued through the year, and it is earnestly hoped that all interested in this movement will give it their cordial support.

1895.

This placard advertised that the first Episcopal service in Milton was to take place on September 29, 1895 in Fraternity Hall in the Associates Building in Milton Village. The preacher on that momentous day was Reverend Charles Tileston Whittemore, Rector of All Saints' Church in Dorchester. September 29th is Michaelmas, the feast of St. Michael the Archangel, and "These services will be continued throughout the year, and it is earnestly hoped that all interested in this movement will give it their cordial support."

The Right Reverend William Lawrence was graduated from Harvard College and Harvard Divinity School. He was elected the 7th Bishop of the Episcopal Diocese of Massachusetts, serving from 1893 to 1927. During that time he was an indefatigable fundraiser for the Episcopal Diocese. In fact, he was quoted as having said, "In the long run it is only to the man of morality that wealth comes... We, like the Psalmists, occasionally see the wicked prosper, but only occasionally. Godliness is in league with riches."

The ground breaking and laying of the cornerstone of St. Michael's Church was held on September 29, 1898 on a lot acquired from the Russell Family that fronted onto Randolph Avenue, and was attended by the Right Reverend William Lawrence. Before ground was broken, Ellen M. Wilde and her sister Anne Doane Wilde Daniell went one evening with a lantern to the lot and held a private prayer service of consecration at the spot where the chancel would stand. Though the church was to be built in Milton, many who attended the ceremonies came out from town on the Dorchester and Milton Branch of the Old Colony Railroad to Milton Village. After an informal reception at the Gannett House, people could return on the train to Boston.

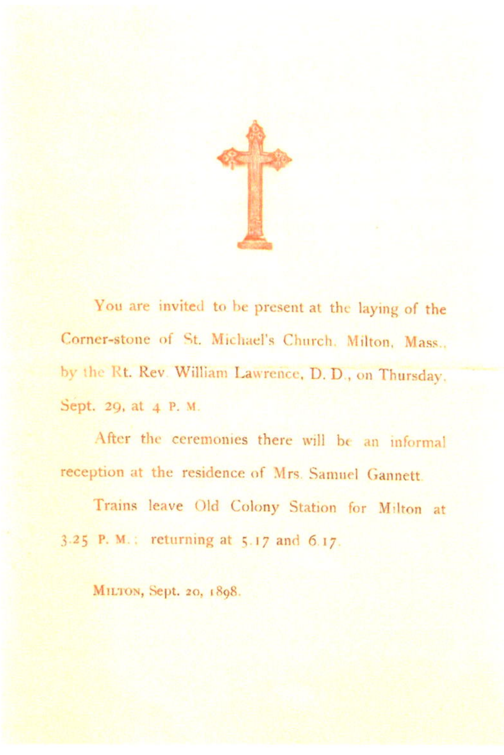

You are invited to be present at the laying of the Corner-stone of St. Michael's Church, Milton, Mass., by the Rt. Rev. William Lawrence, D. D., on Thursday, Sept. 29, at 4 P. M.

After the ceremonies there will be an informal reception at the residence of Mrs. Samuel Gannett.

Trains leave Old Colony Station for Milton at 3.25 P. M.; returning at 5.17 and 6.17.

MILTON, Sept. 20, 1898.

This ink sketch of St. Michael's Church by William Ralph Emerson was done in 1898 with not just a façade elevation but also a proposed floor plan sketch. Emerson's career had been impressive and according to Douglass Shand-Tucci, Emerson was the "Boston architect who most scholars would agree was chiefly responsible for at least the initial development of the Shingle Style of house." As an architect, Emerson was well respected but he was also a noted artist in pencil and pastel. With many years as a successful independent architect, William Ralph Emerson maintained a well-connected Boston base with memberships in the American Institute of Architects, the Boston Society of Architects, the Boston Athenaeum and the Union Club. He was erudite, educated and well informed. He "lived on the gentler side of life, with books and art and the higher interests of his city, and Boston owes him much."

William Ralph Emerson, in a portrait by Dennis Sheehan, trained in the office of Jonathan Preston. In 1857, Emerson and Preston formed an architectural partnership which lasted four years; in 1864 he partnered with Carl Fehmer and they continued as partners for nine years. In 1871 Emerson, with Carl Fehmer, designed the impressive Receiving Tomb at Forest Hills Cemetery. Emerson initially designed in the classical revival style, of which his Post Office and Courthouse in Portland, Maine were early examples. By 1875 he was designing impressive structures that embraced Victorian elements such as the "Shingle Style" architecture that emulated the shingled surfaces of colonial buildings, with the use of gambrel roofs, projecting dormers and wide piazzas. It was said that "country houses were his specialty, and many of the more noteworthy at Bar Harbor and Newport were designed by him." Though Emerson was part of the city and its greater metropolis, he designed impressive residences in Milton, among them *The Pines*, the home of Frances and Margaret Forbes which was considered the premier "Stick Style" house, the Eustis and Tileston houses, houses on Milton Hill and his own house on Randolph Avenue. (Author's collection)

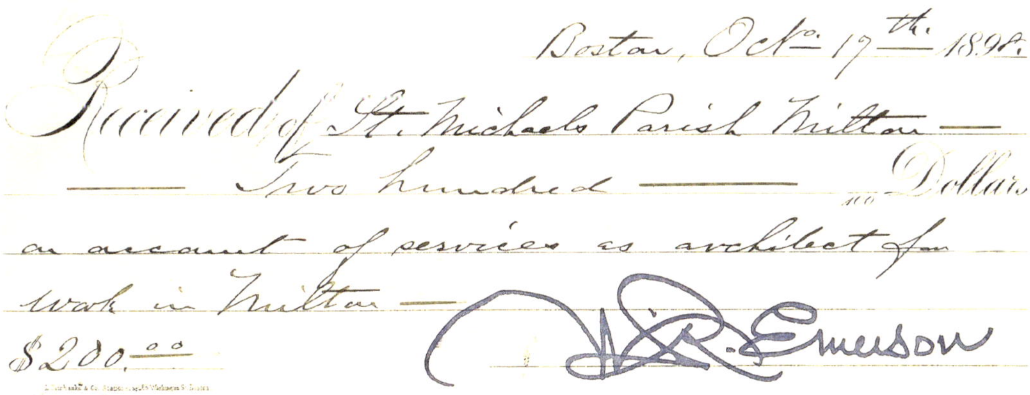

Boston, Oct. 17th 1898.

Received of St. Michaels Parish Milton —

— Two hundred — 00/100 Dollars

on account of services as architect for

work in Milton —

$200.00

W. R. Emerson

This receipt, signed by William Ralph Emerson in 1898, was for "an account of services as architect for work in Milton." Emerson was a leading architect in Boston and was to become known as the "Father of Shingle Style Architecture" and he was eventually paid the grand sum of $350.00 for his design services for the church. However, according to his obituary in the Massachusetts Charitable Mechanics Association Necrology, which he joined in 1856, he was also "a noted painter as well as an architect; pastel was his favorite medium, but he loved to experiment, and the many pictures he left behind testify to his talent and skill. Many people will remember his remarkable ability to draw with both hands at the same time."

The Rector, Wardens and Vestry of Saint Michael's Parish, Milton, Massachusetts, invite you to be present at the Consecration of Saint Michael's Church, on Sunday, October the first, at half past ten o'clock.

Preacher,

The Rt. Rev. William Lawrence, D.D.

The invitation to the Consecration of St. Michael's Church was for ceremonies to be held on October 1, 1905, with Bishop William Lawrence preaching. A canon enacted in 1868 required that the church and its grounds be fully paid for and free of debt or legal encumbrances before it could be consecrated. With the debt and mortgage paid within a decade, the church was on firm financial footing and had grown tremendously over the last decade.

An early twentieth-century photograph of St. Michael's Church from Randolph Avenue shows the impressive random ashlar stone church with mature plantings and the façade covered in ivy. The cornerstone of St. Michael's Church is engraved with a Canterbury Cross with the date AD MDCCCXCVIII (1898) and was provided by John Heuss of Willard Street, West Quincy for $25.00. (Author's collection)

Sir Everard Alexander Hambro, KCVO JP DL (1842–1925), was the Lord of the Manor of Milton Abbas. His family hailed from Denmark and his father, Carl Joachim Hambro, founded Hambros Bank in London in 1839. Sir Everard not only was head of Hambros Bank but served on the Board of Directors of the Bank of England from 1879 to 1925. It was Hambro who, at the request of Reverend Theodore Reese, donated the stone from Milton Abbas that was to be used at St. Michael's Church. (Author's collection)

This Norman stone came from the Milton Abbey in Milton Abbas, Dorset England at the request of Reverend Theodore Reese, St. Michael's first Lay Reader and Rector from 1898 to 1907. The stone was given "as a witness of the common faith of this church with the Church of England and to the historic associations which unite these two towns of Milton in Old and New England." The stone from Milton Abbey in Milton Abbas, England arrived in 1904 and was installed as the keystone over the inner archway entrance to St. Michael's Church. Milton Abbey has retained close ties with St. Michael's Church ever since.

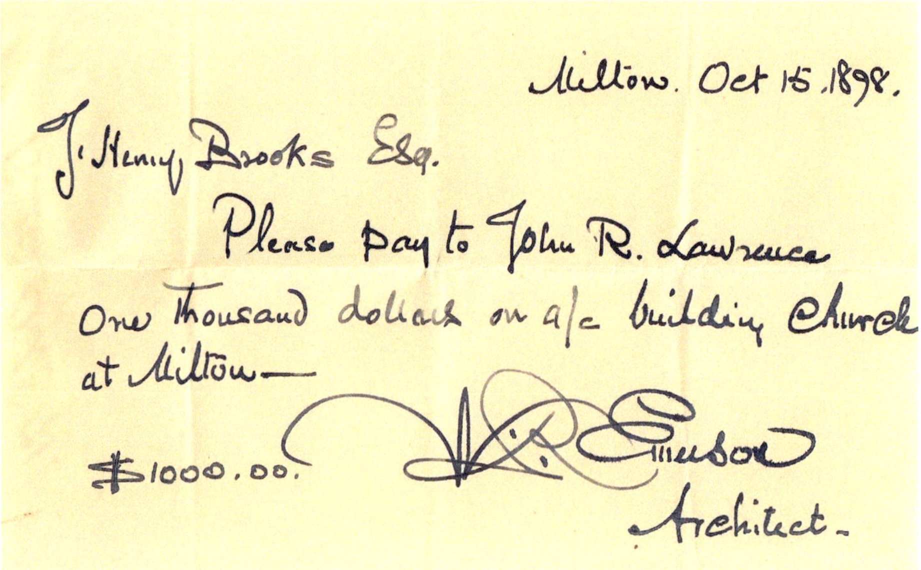

Milton. Oct 15, 1898.

J. Henry Brooks Esq.

Please pay to John R. Lawrence
One thousand dollars on a/c building Church
at Milton—

$1000.00 W. R. Emerson
Architect.

An 1898 receipt from William Ralph Emerson was sent to J. Henry Brooks, then Treasurer of St. Michael's Church, to pay local builder John R. Lawrence the sum of $1,000.00 on account for "building church in Milton." Lawrence, engaged in the general contracting business in Milton, built many houses in Milton. His obituary in the *Milton Record* said "His business outside the town was also extensive and he had been engaged in the erection of prominent churches and other public buildings in the vicinity."

St. Michael's Church is one of William Ralph Emerson's most engaging designs. Built of local seam-faced granite blocks laid in a random ashlar design, it evokes a sense of an English village church on Randolph Avenue. The crenelated battlement tower, with its lancet-arched entrance-side stained glass window, and louvered screens in the tower, was originally devised so that warriors might protect a medieval castle by discharging arrows or other missiles through the crenels. The battlement was to be used in architecture as a solid pile of stone protecting the word of God.

The chancel in the original St. Michael's Church was a barrel-vaulted arch of white painted stucco, with the altar designed by John Evans. The first service in the new church was on Easter Sunday 1899 and one can imagine the immense pride that the parishioners felt with the church now ready to have services after three years at Fraternity Hall. Reverend Theodore Reese preached that morning, and the text of his sermon was "To know Thee is perfect service."

> I beseech you therefore, brethren, by the mercies of God, that ye present your bodies as living sacrifice, holy, acceptable unto God, which is your reasonable service.
>
> Romans 12:1

Looking along the nave of the church towards the chancel with the three arches was a starkly simple design with massive wood framing creating an intimate space in which to worship God. It is thought that this photograph is from Easter 1899 as the altar, with a large brass cross by Gorham Company, is decorated with Easter lilies and the chancel with evergreens and spring flowers. It was said in the church records that "it was a joyous congregation that met to worship for the first time in the new church."

On June 1, 1914, Charlotte Fellowes Harding and Walter Keese Earle were married at St. Michael's Church. The flowers used to decorate the church for the wedding ceremony were planned by Mrs. George Wigglesworth and included white birch, deutzia, and spirea. On the right in the side archway is the original two-manual organ with pedals that was installed by Kimball, Smallman and Frazee; the first organist was Perkins F. Smith, author of *Perkins' Model Class-Book*. The chandeliers, fixtures and lamps were installed by McKenney & Waterbury Company of Boston, manufacturers and jobbers of gas, electric and combination fixtures.

The Chancel, with its white draped backdrop and brass cross, was beautifully decorated for the Harding-Earle wedding with hanging smilax framing the barrel vault arch, masses of flowers flanking the altar as well as the chandeliers, and each pew decorated with a nosegay of flowers. The bride was the daughter of Benjamin Fosdick and Lucy Williams Harding and the groom was the son of Oliver Keese and Emma Tyler Earle.

3

Architectural History

Know ye not that ye are the temple of God, and that the Spirit of God dwelleth in you?

1 Corinthians 3:16

A photograph from the early 1920s shows St. Michael's Church with the Parish House on the far right. In 1910, it had been voted by the Vestry: "That the building committee be authorized to proceed with the plans which have been submitted by the architectural firm of Cram and Ferguson of Boston, for a Parish House." Cram and Ferguson was a noted architectural firm that would transform St. Michael's Church from a small suburban church into one that was not only impressive but embellished with important commissions from stone carvers, wood carvers and stained-glass artists who united to create a veritable temple of God. The grounds, after the 1917 expansion, were graded by John M. Reynolds Company.

Ralph Adams Cram (1863–1942) was considered one of the foremost architects of the turn of the twentieth century. He worked for five years in the offices of Rotch and Tilden and founded his own architectural practice in 1889. After a series of partners, the architectural firm became known as Cram and Ferguson Architects in 1913. In 1915 Cram spoke before members of St. Michael's Church on his ideas as to the expansion the church, and according to the Minutes, "explaining the fine opportunity for enlarging the church so that the proper space should be given to the chancel and choir stalls." His suggestion that the sides of the chancel, sanctuary and the ceiling be in dark oak with grey walls which were painted by Bates & Swanson Company was a resounding success.

The expansion of the church in 1916 increased seating, which was commissioned from the American Seating Company in Grand Rapids, which also provided the chancel paneling and choir stalls. The sides of the chancel and sanctuary were paneled in dark oak and the altar was designed by Alexander Hoyle, an architect with Cram and Ferguson, from a fifteenth-century English Gothic design. Johannes Kirchmeyer of William F. Ross & Company of Roxbury carved the altar screen and reredos. Kirchmeyer was trained in sculpture in Germany and after immigrating to the United States received encouragement from Sanford White, Henry Vaughan, Ralph Adams Cram and other architects, as well as from the management of the Boston Society of Arts and Crafts, of which he became a master craftsman. He was later employed by Irving & Casson and worked on many of the buildings of the noted American Gothic revivalist Ralph Adams Cram.

This photograph shows the altar, reredos and Lockwood memorial window after its completion in 1916. The altar was designed by John Evans, a Welsh sculptor who first worked with H.H. Richardson on the completion of the Bartholi frieze on the tower of the Brattle Square (now First Baptist) Church in Boston. Evans was a member of the Society of Arts and Crafts in Boston, and a prominent member of Boston's medieval "guild" of artists. He collaborated with Ralph Adams Cram to create an impressive design in the new and enlarged chancel. John Boltz was a native of Germany who carved the pulpit and lectern. Notice the two twisted columns supporting gilded statues of angels which hold candles on either side of the altar. The finely carved reredos was by Johannes Kirchmeyer and the panels were designed by Mary Young-Hunter, a well-known painter who often exhibited with the Royal Academy of Arts in London. Her works Joy and the Labourer, Olivia, and Where Shall Wisdom be Found? were included in the book *Women Painters of the World*. Among the altar pieces is a brass bible stand engraved "Easter Sunday 1899," a brass donation plate given in 1899 in memory of Bertha Lyman Brooks, and altar chairs given in memory of Harriet L. Gannett.

The Right Reverend William Lawrence consecrated the renovations to St. Michael's Church on Passion Sunday, April 1, 1917. Over the previous three years, the planning process and designs drawn by Ralph Adams Cram greatly enlarged the church but also, according to Reverend H. Boyd Edwards, Rector from 1913–1921, "The recent enlargement of the Church includes an addition to the nave, transept, chancel and sanctuary." In the *Church Militant* in April 1917, it was said of "Milton's Beautified Church" that Cram and Ferguson "have achieved a fine result not only in dignity, symmetry and simplicity of its general construction but also in refinement, harmony, softness and repose of the interior."

Ralph Adams Cram was to literally transform St. Michael's Church from a small suburban church into one that was an architectural landmark. As Rev. Edwards said, the "general style of architecture is a modern [1917] handling of English Perpendicular Gothic. In every detail the work is completely satisfactory to the whole congregation." Cram had been appointed architect for the Cathedral of St. John the Divine in New York and was so highly regarded that he appeared on the cover of TIME Magazine on December 13, 1926 (Volume VIII, No. 24.) His biography said: "Cram was converted to Anglo-Catholicism as a young man...[and] was so attached to the medieval way of life that nearly all of his voluminous writings [*My Life in Architecture, The End of Democracy*] were concerned with his vision of its resurgence." His dream included a return of self-sufficient walled towns, a return of craftsmen's guilds and an abolition of mass production." (Courtesy of Cram and Ferguson Architects, with thanks to Ethan Anthony)

Seen in 1918, St. Michael's Church and the Parish Hall, on the right, designed by Cram and Ferguson, had greatly enlarged not only the seating capacity from 200 to 420 seats in the church but also meeting and office space. Reverend H. Boyd Edwards said in a sermon that the work of Cram and Ferguson was not only successful but that "the refinement, harmony, softness and repose of the interior" pleased not just himself but the entire congregation.

The simple wood-framed dormer entrance to the side of the church was added by Cram and Ferguson in 1917. With random ashlar piers as supports to the wood timbers and an open wood design, it was a good example of Ralph Adams Cram's interpretation of what he called English Perpendicular Gothic. (Photo by Peter B. Kingman)

Ralph Lincoln Emerson (1868–1899) was the son of the noted architect William Ralph Emerson and Katherine Varnum Mears Emerson. Ralph L. Emerson prepared at Hopkinson's School on Beacon Hill and was graduated from Harvard University in 1891, after which he served as a draftsman in his father's architectural office. He was unwell in the late 1890s and went to Atlanta, Georgia to recuperate. There he was married to Lillias Caroline Stephenson on April 14, 1899, and Emerson died the following day. In his obituary in the *St. Paul Globe* on April 19, 1899, it said "At the time of the marriage it was known that Mr. Emerson must die in a very short time, but both he and Miss Stephenson wished the marriage to take place." (Author's collection)

The Rectory of St. Michael's Church was designed by William Ralph Emerson, assisted by his son Ralph Lincoln Emerson, who was working as a draftsman in his father's office. It was one of at least a dozen houses that Emerson was to design for Milton residents, many of whom he was related to by marriage to his second wife Sylvia Hathaway Watson Emerson. With its asymmetrical design with a center porch flanked by a large bay window, the wood Shingle Style house fit into its suburban location well and was an unobtrusive foil to the impressive random ashlar stone church.

This bas-relief of St. Michael the Archangel was given by Sylvia Hathaway Watson Emerson in memory of her stepson Ralph Lincoln Emerson, who participated in the design of the original church building along with his father, architect William Ralph Emerson. Sadly, Ralph L. Emerson died in 1899 at the age of 31, the same year both buildings were completed. First installed in the original church, the bas-relief was moved to its current location after the church was enlarged in 1916 by the addition of the chapel and the chancel, choir stalls and altar area and sacristy. The architect for that work was Ralph Adams Cram, whose firm, Cram and Ferguson, had also designed the Parish House, completed in 1911. The bas-relief was restored in 2020 by Jean-Louis Lachevre. (Photo by Peter B. Kingman)

This Caproni Cast is The Madonna and Child and is a depiction in half-length of Mary holding Jesus, who is shown in profile and seated before her on a cushion. Jesus touches her left wrist with his left hand and, in delicately sculpted detail, holds up her veil with his right hand. It is thought that the original marble relief was made in the style of Florentine sculptor Desiderio da Settignano (c.1429–1464). This plaster cast was done from the original in the Victoria and Albert Museum in London by Pietro Paulo Caproni (1862–1928) who was founder and co-owner with his brother Emilio Caproni of P.P. Caproni & Brother in Roxbury, manufacturers of plaster reproductions of classical and contemporary statues. The cast hangs in the Associate Rector's office.

The Memorial Chapel contains the original altar from the church that was moved by Cram and Ferguson and reset by the John Evans Company in 1917, and a kneeler that was given in memory of Martha Linette Richardson (1848–1924). Miss Richardson not only taught Sunday School classes at the church from 1899 onward, but she "had a class of girls who felt that her teaching made a turning point in their lives." She was a member of St. Michael's Guild from 1902 to 1908, serving as president in 1902 and 1903; she also served as secretary of the Milton Convalescent Home and the Milton Social Service League and was a member of the Milton Women's Club.

A detail of the hand carved figure on the Richardson kneeler in the Memorial Chapel shows the intricacy of the carving by Johannes Kirchmeyer, who was awarded the Craftsmanship Medal for Distinguished Achievement in Wood Carving by the American Institute of Architects. This simple but delightful carving was given to the Glory of God and in memory of Martha Linette Richardson. Reverend Vincent LeRoy Bennett said of her that "she was one of the founders of St. Michael's Parish, whose generosity and devotion helped to build this church; whose loyalty was expressed in energetic work; who worked on despite impaired health; who gave to us despite her declining strength until she had no more to give; a rare soul whose life is an immortal blessing to this parish."

A c. 1912 color postcard shows St. Michael's Church set on a slight knoll overlooking Randolph Avenue, with its stone facade covered with English ivy. A truly bucolic setting for the impressive church.

In whom all the building fitly framed together groweth unto an holy temple in the Lord

Ephesians 2:21

St. Michael's Church, seen from the side, shows the church in 1920 with its crenelated battlement tower surmounted by a low conical roof. Though Emerson had sketched a cock at the top of the roof, it was never installed. The great west window, seen on the facade, was known as the Bennett Memorial Window, given to the Glory of God and in memory of Edna Henry Bennett, wife of Reverend Vincent L. Bennett. The window was made by James Ballentine and Son of Edinburgh, Scotland, that had designed windows for the House of Lords, Parliament in London. It is a three-part lancet-arched window, which has three resurrection scenes: the center panel depicts Mary Magdalene and the risen Christ, the left the Tomb of Golgotha with Mary, Salome and Mary Magdalene and the right the supper at Emmaus.

And it came to pass, as He sat at meat with them, He took bread and blessed it, and broke and gave it to them. And their eyes were opened and they knew Him. And He vanished out of their sight.

Luke 24: 30-31

Three early members of St. Michael's Church were, from left to right: J. Henry Brooks (1844–1913), Lucretia Gilbert Brooks (1848–1933), and James H. Ricketson (1854–1907). John Henry Brooks served as Treasurer of the Church from 1898 to 1906 and lived at *Wayside Farm* on Adams Street in Milton. He was a partner with John Murray Forbes in the Chicago, Burlington and Quincy Railroad, and the Michigan Central Railroad. James H. Ricketson was a well-known tenor soloist, having studied in London with George Henschel, who in 1881 became the first conductor of the Boston Symphony Orchestra. For many years he was the tenor soloist at the Arlington Street Church in Boston, and a vocal teacher at his home in Milton. One wonders what the doffing of their bowler hats was in reaction to!

James Hattrick Lee (1843–1903) was ordained a deacon in the Episcopal church in 1869 and served as the Senior Warden at St. Michael's Church from 1896 to 1903. He was a Master at Milton Academy and a respected collector of classical Greek pottery. He died in Rome while on the Grand Tour with his wife Abigail Eloise Stearns Lee. As Reverend Reese said in his funeral sermon, which was published In Memory of James Hattrick Lee: A Sermon Delivered in St. Michael's Church on Trinity Sunday: "These words come from that great catalogue of heroes which constitutes the eleventh chapter of the Epistle to the Hebrews. In vivid pictures the heroes of mankind, from the dawn of history, are marshaled before our eyes; to each is given some personal touch, some terse phrase, which proclaims the lofty ideal which has been his inspiration and made him worthy to be called God's workman."

Benjamin Fosdick Harding (1857–1923) served as Senior Warden from 1903 to 1923. He was graduated from Harvard and served as a tutor at St. Mark's School, and later taught at St. Paul's School, Hopkinson School and the Belmont School for Boys, which he founded and personally financed. He was later a Senior Master at Milton Academy, where he and his wife Lucy Lambert Williams Harding nurtured a generation of students. He published Greek Inflection: *Or, Object-Lessons in Greek Philology*. Annually Milton Academy awards the Benjamin Fosdick Harding Latin Prizes, which are given on the basis of a separate test at each prize level. He was an editor of the *Harvard Graduates' Magazine* and later served as an Overseer of Harvard. One thing that proves he was a true Renaissance man was that he received a patent in 1911 for an ash can attachment!

George Marston Cushing served as Treasurer of St. Michael's Church from 1923 to 1946. He was graduated from Hopkinson School and Harvard, as well as Harvard Law School. He said in his 25th Anniversary Report in 1919: "My first year in the practice of the law was spent in the office of R. M. Saltonstall, Esq., where the work was active and interesting. The following year [Elias Bullard] Bishop, '94, and I became partners, and we have continued practicing law together [as Cushing & Bishop] with offices at 54 Devonshire Street, Boston." He was married to Grace Littleton Cushing and was a member of the Somerset Club, Union Club, Automobile Club of Boston, New Riding Club, Norfolk Hunt Club, Hoosic-Whisick Club, and the Boston Bar Association.

The Rectory of St. Michael's Church was designed by William Ralph Emerson, assisted by his son Ralph Lincoln Emerson who was then working in the office as a draftsman, and was built in 1899 adjacent to the church. A large Shingle Style house, it was originally built on the site of the present driveway and was moved just south in 1954. Notice the porch and dormer of the Village School on the far right. Purchased from Milton Academy in 1951, the school building had been used as the Lower School with a Children's Chapel.

To create an open flank to St. Michael's Church, the parish decided to move the Rectory to the lot adjacent to it, which had been purchased in 1951. Alanson Sturgis of Sturgis Associates, Inc. oversaw the moving and both exterior and interior renovations done to the Rectory. Seen here jacked up on a frame, the house would be moved to the foundation in the foreground.

4

The Stained Glass Windows

People are like stained-glass windows. They sparkle and shine when the sun is out, but when the darkness sets in, their true beauty is revealed only if there is a light from within.

Elisabeth Kubler-Ross

The center part of the Reynolds Memorial window depicts St. Michael the Archangel, with the theme of the window taken from St. Paul's Epistles as expressed in the quotation from Ephesians 6:13: "Take unto you the whole armour of God."

A Collect for St. Michael and All Angels:

Everlasting God, you have ordained and constituted in a wonderful order the ministries of angels and mortals: Mercifully grant that, as your holy angels always serve and worship you in heaven, so by your appointment they may help and defend us here on earth; through Jesus Christ our Lord, who lives and reigns with you and the Holy Spirit, one God, for ever and ever.

Amen

The Lockwood Memorial window is prominently placed above the altar. The reredos, altar rail and cross vases were given in 1916 by Julia M. Fairbanks to the Glory of God and in memory of her parents Charles and Julia Missroon Fairbanks. The panels of the beautifully carved reredos have on the top from left to right: St. George, St. Peter, St. Paul and St. Michael. On the bottom from left to right: Angel Gabriel, Blessed Virgin Mary, St. John and St. Andrew. The center panel is of the Ascending Christ. These panels were created by the noted artist Mary Young-Hunter and were of carved wood covered with linen, laid down with marine glue and then plastered before being painted. (Photo by Peter B. Kingman)

The Lockwood Memorial window was designed by Ralph Adams Cram and dedicated to the Glory of God and in memory of Rhodes and Henrietta Niles Lockwood in 1917. The window was donated by their daughter Emily Niles Lockwood Wood, who lived on Milton Hill. Rhodes Lockwood was president and treasurer of the Davidson Rubber Company. Founded by his grandfather Charles H. Davidson, it was a successful manufacturer of rubber goods for druggists, surgeons, and other specialized concerns. He lived in Boston's Back Bay and had a summer house in Lexington. (Photo by Peter B. Kingman)

> Wait on the Lord, be of good course, and he shall strengthen thine heart.
>
> Psalm 27:14

Ralph Adams Cram (1863–1942) is considered the foremost Gothic revival architect in the United States. Inspired by the influential English critic John Ruskin, Cram became an advocate of and an authority on English and French Gothic styles and introduced them to Boston through his many ecclesiastical commissions, among them St. Michael's Church. In 1889, he established an architectural firm (Cram & Wentworth) with Charles Francis Wentworth, where he practiced with a series of partners, including Bertram Goodhue (Cram, Wentworth & Goodhue) and F.W. Ferguson (Cram, Goodhue & Ferguson.) Cram headed the architecture department of the Massachusetts Institute of Technology for seven years, and was as successful in imparting his skill as was William Rotch Ware of Milton, who preceded him as the first head. Together with the architect Richard Upjohn and artist John LaFarge, Cram is honored on December 16th by a feast day in the Episcopal Church of the United States.

A detail of the Epistle Panel of the Lockwood Memorial window shows St. George, St. Augustine, St. Helena, St. Francis and St. Martin of Tours. The profile of St. Augustine, depicted in a gentle golden circle, is said to be Ralph Adams Cram (unfortunately now obscured by a reinforcing saddle rod). Cram was a member of the Church of the Advent on Beacon Hill and a high church Episcopalian. Walter Muir Whitehill said of his likeness in 1964 that "the absence of an enormous pair of horn-rimmed spectacles, which was the most conspicuous part of his face, makes the likeness a little less striking than one would anticipate. Also, the substitution of a miter for a bowler hat makes a certain amount of difference." (Photo by Peter B. Kingman)

The Reynolds Memorial Window was given to the Glory of God and in memory of Phillip Murray and Mary Blaisdell Gardner Reynolds in 1924 by their children Harrison Gardner Reynolds, James Robbins Reynolds and Barbara Murray Reynolds Burnett. This impressive triptych-stained glass window was designed and made by the Studio of Joseph G. Reynolds & Associates of Charlestown and states "Take Unto You the Whole Armour of God." The center panel depicts St. Michael the Archangel in a suit of armor with his shield bearing the sun overlayed by a red cross. The left panel is of St. Paul holding a great sword and the right panel depicts St. Prisca, who with her husband Aquilla lived in Rome, working as tent makers with St. Paul, who was instrumental in her conversion and martyrdom. (Photo by Peter B. Kingman)

> Wherefore take unto you the whole armour of God, that ye may be able to withstand in the evil day, and having done all, to stand. Stand therefore, having your loins girt about with truth, and having on the breastplate of righteousness. And your feet shod with the preparation of the gospel of peace. Above all, taking the shield of faith, wherewith ye shall be able to quench all the fiery darts of the wicked. And take the helmet of salvation, and the sword of the Spirit, which is the word of God.
>
> Ephesians 6:13-17

Mary Blaisdell Gardner Reynolds and Philip Murray Reynolds are seen sitting on their piazza in Milton. Mr. Reynolds had served as the first Treasurer of St. Michael's Church and Mrs. Reynolds had served as President of the Women of St. Michael's Church. Reynolds prepared at G.W.C. Noble's School and was graduated from Harvard in 1889; he was an attorney and was associated with Thomson-Houston Electric Company, General Electric Company, Brown Electric Company and Anchor Electric Company and treasurer of the Ipswich Mills. He was also treasurer of the Old Colony and the Boston and Northern Street Railway Companies.

Above left: The Lee Memorial Window was a twin panel window given by James Hattrick Lee in 1900 to the Glory of God and in memory of Henry Howey Lee and William Frazer Lee, and was the first stained glass window at St. Michael's. It was replaced in 1960 with a new one designed by Wilbur Herbert Burnham which was in memory of the Early Members of This Parish, 1895 to 1907. This window depicts the baptism of Jesus Christ in the Jordan River by John the Baptist, the Angel Gabriel as a messenger of God, and the Holy Spirit, depicted as a white dove. This window was not just to honor the Byers, Cooke, Cushing, Gannett, Herrick, Hollis, Jackson, Lee, Reynolds, Richardson, Stevens, Whitney and Wilde families but also those whose names were not well known and were recorded in the church records as early members of the church. (Photo by Peter B. Kingman)

Above right: Wilbur Herbert Burnham, seen in his studio, created the new Parish Window in 1960, dedicated to the Glory of God and in memory of the early parishioners of St. Michael's Church on the 65th anniversary of the church. He began his career as a stained glass artist in 1904 and opened his own studio in 1922, working with Charles J. Connick and Joseph C. Reynolds. Burnham Studios became recognized as one of the most prominent stained glass design companies in the United States. He was commissioned by Ralph Adams Cram to design windows in the early twentieth century and, as an advocate of the medieval stained glass tradition, Burnham's philosophical compatibilities with those of the enormously successful Cram led to a commission to provide a window for St. Michael's Church in 1916. Burnham served as president of the Stained Glass Association of America from 1938–1941. (Archives of American Art, Smithsonian Institution)

The Wilde Memorial Window was given to the Glory of God and in memory of Ellen Maria Wilde (1841–1919) by the congregation in 1920. Depicted are Jesus and the Syrophoenician woman before the cities of Tyre and Sidon. Ellen Wilde was not just a devoted member of St. Michael's Church but the person who spearheaded its being established by the Episcopal Diocese. Reverend Reese said of her: " St. Michael's Parish owes to this woman of faith, a great debt. Her life is built into the eternal structure of the parish life, remaining through the generations a constant inspiration to keep the faith in which the Church was built and by which it stands." Ellen Wilde was the daughter of Henry Jackson and Ellen Whitney Wilde and a granddaughter of Judge Samuel Sumner Wilde, Associate Justice of the Massachusetts Supreme Judicial Court.

Then Jesus answered and said unto her, O woman, great is thy faith: be it unto thee even as thou wilt.

Matthew 15:28

Charles Jay Connick (1875–1945) was a prominent American painter, muralist, and designer best known for his work in stained glass in the Gothic Revival style. Cram said that he was "clever in adapting ancient methods to modern requirements." His stained glass studio at 9 Harcourt Street in Boston was the arts and crafts ideal in that the art was produced by a community of committed and highly skilled craftsmen. In the early 1930s, an average of fifty men and women worked at the studio and produced impressive windows for both ecclesiastical as well as residential commissions. Founded on the principles of a medieval craft guild, the studio was closely allied with Ralph Adams Cram, dean of the Gothic Revival in American architecture.

Charles J. Connick drew and illustrated in watercolor a design for the twin stained-glass windows proposed in memory of Alfred Rogers, Jr. Connick was a brilliant artist and in his book *Adventures in Light and Color: An Introduction to the Stained Glass Craft*, he discusses how he approaches the characteristics of stained-glass art and its impact from ancient European glass to the present. The general feel and color on his windows at St. Michael's give an impression of the traditional with even more opalescence than the original windows of centuries ago. Upon his death, The *New York Times* reported that Connick was "considered the world's greatest artisan on stained windows."

The Rogers Memorial window was given by Alfred and Susan Hardy Barnes Rogers to the Glory of God and in memory of their son Alfred Rogers Jr. (1912–1942) who was killed during World War II. The window was designed by Charles Jay Connick and completed and installed in 1944. The scene depicts Jesus raising the son of the widow of Nain. Jesus and his followers are seen on the left and the widow and her son on the right. (Photo by Peter B. Kingman)

> This is my beloved son in whom I am well pleased.
>
> Matthew 3:17

Jim Anderson of Jim Anderson Stained Glass in Boston's South End and Lisa Elliott, the main craftsperson who cut the glass, created the new stained glass window dedicated to the Women of St. Michael's. As Reverend Hall Kirkham said in the 2019 Annual Report: "The great gift I received this year, from the spirit of great legacies in this community, was the chance to witness the Women of St. Michael's window come from an idea into a reality, and it graces our worship space today not just with light and life streaming into the chapel, but with the proclamation that St. Michael's honors the care and commitment of its family members, distant as well as current. The window speaks to the unsung everywhere—here and outside these walls—who are the backbone of the ministries we boast: outreach, education, parish life, care for our grounds and building, and worship and guilds. It is an astonishingly beautiful tribute to an astonishingly powerful tradition."

Jim Anderson said of the new stained-glass window that was given to the Glory of God and in honor of the Women of St. Michael's and which embraces the flora and fauna of Milton with a doe, rabbit, turkey, chipmunk and a variety of birds as well as an owl at the very top and masses of snowdrops and blue scilla: "I designed the stained glass to give a view of the women's garden outside. I thought it would be nice to appreciate the garden through the different seasons so the stained glass becomes a frame for the ever-changing nature outside." (Photo by Peter B. Kingman)

5

Music Program

Let the word of Christ dwell in you richly; teach and admonish one another in all wisdom; and with gratitude in your hearts sing psalms, hymns, and spiritual songs to God.

Colossians 3:16

The Bible has never said "let those who have beautiful voices sing," as if natural talent were a requirement to praise God! Psalm 95:1 says "Oh come, let us sing to the Lord; let us make a joyful noise to the rock of our salvation! Let us come into his presence with thanksgiving; let us make a joyful noise to him with songs of praise!" So just sing! Over and over, dozens of times, we are commanded to sing: sing to the Lord, sing praises, sing joyfully, sing a new song. Come into God's presence with singing. Here Mavis Young, Elizabeth Schmellick, and Eileen Rush sing joyfully as part of the choir of St. Michael's.

The members of the St. Michael's Choir pose for a group photograph in the late 1920s with the women wearing flowing robes with white linen collars and caps and the men wearing a surplice over a plain black cassock. Seen in the front row, from left to right: Madeleine Vasseur Henderson, Dorothy Maskell, Eleanor King Johnson, Mrs. Freeman, unknown, unknown, Mrs. Pickett, unknown. In the second row from left to right are: unknown, Mr. Burgess, Tony, a blind tenor, unknown, unknown, Henry King, the Crucifer, unknown, Reverend Vincent L. Bennett, Harold L. Pickett, church organist, Arleen Hersey Batting, unknown.

Lauriston Livingston Scaife (1907–1970), seen in 1915, was a young parishioner who participated in the boys' choir and was confirmed at St. Michael's in 1923. Son of Roger Livingston and Ethel May Bryant Scaife, he prepared at Milton Academy and was graduated from Trinity College. He studied at the General Theological Seminary and graduated with a Bachelor of Sacred Theology in 1938 and a Doctor of Divinity from Trinity in 1948. Between 1937 and 1938, he served as Master of St. Paul's School in Concord, New Hampshire. In 1938 he became the assistant priest of Saint Thomas' Church in New York City and in 1942 he became rector of Trinity Church in Newport, Rhode Island. In 1948, Scaife was elected Bishop of Western New York.

The St. Michael's Boys' Choir, followed by members of the Adult Choir, are seen processing to the church entrance in 1919. The tradition of a boys' choir has long been a major part of Episcopal worship and dates to the late nineteenth century, with many of the boys singing tenor, alto or bass and the younger ones, technically known as trebles, singing soprano. The older boys and men would sing the lower parts.

St. Michael's Junior Choir poses for a group photograph in 1958. The young acolyte in the center rear, flanked by acolytes wearing cassocks, holds the processional cross that was given to the Glory of God by James H. Ricketson. These obviously happy members of the Junior Choir often learned important skills in addition to singing, such as citizenship, patience, self-discipline, ability to focus, and good humor.

Preparing for church are Alice "Allie" Brown Graves, Barbara "Barbie" Harding Feather, Mary Sweitzer Pierce, Elizabeth "Cheeky" Perkins Draper and, seen in the mirror, Ginny Marr.

St. Michael's Choir is seen posing for a group photograph in the choir of the church. In the back row, from left to right are Stephen Weld, Larry Gall, Steve Wilson, George Corbett, Richard Jackmauh, Barratt Park, Fred Carter; in the middle are Anne Wood, Lana Agnew, Dina Roberts Bray, Marilyn Cheney, Joan Faulkner, Rebecca Richardson; in the front are Britt Brown, Patricia Vanston and Katherine Ware.

Serve the Lord with gladness: come before his presence with singing.

Psalms 100:2

Four members the choir of St. Michael's Church who are baritone and bass singers are from left to right, Steve Wilson, Ryne Cherry, a New England Conservatory opera grad student, George Corbett and Larry Gall.

The retirement of John P. Whiteside was a moving occasion. Whiteside was graduated from Colorado College with a Doctorate in Organ Performance. He studied organ with John Ferris, Max Miller, and Anton Heiller and conducting with J. Julius Baird and the late Robert Shaw. He served as Dean of the American Guild of Organists, Boston Chapter, from 1990 to 1992 and was at St. Michael's from 1990 to 2001. He said: "Making music at St. Michael's during the years I was there was an extraordinary experience, largely because of the choir's willingness to tackle new music, and exploring new ways of learning that music. The congregation was exciting as well, and was eager to explore their spiritual growth through many avenues, including music. In that environment we were able to do some astounding things, such as a performance of portions of Sergei Rachmaninoff's All-Night Vigil (Vespers) and Bach's Magnificat, performed during worship in Advent with full orchestral accompaniment." Seen here from left to right are Marilyn Cheney, Rev. Ellie Panasevich, Leah Whiteside, John Whiteside, Ann Whiteside, David Whiteside, Reverend Sam Rodman, Doug Carter, unknown, Charlie Johnson and Claire Higgins.

Frank van Atta began the Cathedral Choir (the Children's Choir), an educational youth choir for treble voices in grades one through eight. He was reaching out to those who love to sing, or enjoy playing an instrument, to participate in the music ministry at St. Michael's. He urged all to sign up to participate in the Summer Music Series and said: "All ages and ability levels are warmly welcomed."

Frank J. Van Atta, seen on the right, served as Organist and Choir Director at St. Michael's Church from 2012 to 2018; during this time, he also was at Brimmer and May as the Director of Middle and Upper School Music. It was said that "Mr. Van Atta brings a wealth of experience as a music educator and choral conductor, demonstrating deep care and exceptional leadership with developing voices," and he was greatly admired by the members of St. Michael's Choir. A reception with a cake sporting a marzipan keyboard served as a sweet thank you from parishioners and friends to bid him Godspeed in his new endeavors.

Todd Beckham, directing the Choir of St. Michael's and an orchestra, is seen in front of the palm-decorated altar; he was at St. Michael's from 2001 to 2011. Beckham was graduated from Youngstown State University as an organ performance major, and from Converse College with a Master of Music in organ and harpsichord performance. He also did postgraduate studies in choral conducting and sacred music at Boston University. He had been harpsichord tutor at Mather house at Harvard University and served as the Director of Meridian Singers at Massachusetts Institute of Technology. He served as Director of Music and organist at The Cathedral of St. Andrew, Honolulu, while he was the Choral Accompanist at Hawaii Pacific University as well as organist at Kamehameha Schools. Mr. Beckham is today the organist and Choirmaster at Christ Church Cathedral in Springfield, Massachusetts.

On Palm Sunday 2010, the Missa brevis in D major, which was composed by Wolfgang Amadeus Mozart and completed in 1774, was sung in the context of the service under the direction of Todd Beckham. The two men in the front row are tenors Barratt Park and Robert Goodrich and behind them is Larry Gall. The orchestra was made up of period instruments with First Violin Guiomar Turgeon, Second Violin Lena Wong, Cello Jane Leggiero, Double Bass unknown, and Positive organ Fred Backhaus. The soloists were Kathy Blixt, soprano, Mary Gerbi, mezzo-soprano, Barratt Park, tenor, and Larry Gall, bass.

A bell was acquired in 2005 with thanks to a very generous benefactor. Funds were donated to acquire the 34-inch diameter 800-pound bronze bell that was cast at the Jones Bell Company of Troy, New York. The bell arrived in Milton on a wood pallet and was being hoisted to the tower. Interestingly, no bell had ever hung in the battlement tower of St. Michael's Church since it was completed in 1899. This bell was purchased from Brosamer Bells, operated by Bob Brosamer, a collector and broker of bells. Seen in this photo in front of the church, the workmen were preparing for the installation of the new bell.

The sound of the bells will be heard when he enters the Holy Place before the Lord, and when he comes out.

Exodus 28:35

Before the bell could be hung, the battlement tower required interior rebuilding and the installation of structural supports; the design work was done by Craig Barnes of CBI Consulting in Boston. The interior masonry of the tower had to be rebuilt to provide for the steel beams to support the bell, which was done by Jeff Lanreville of Millennium Home Improvements in Hanson. The bell is seen suspended in midair attached to its yoke as a crane lifts it to its eventual placement in the church tower.

Marjorie Asfour-Kirkham rings the new bell in the narthex of St. Michael's in front of a wood panel wall that was given in memory of Julia Bourne Thurber (1869–1960). Traditionally, a church bell is used to call worshippers to the church for services, but it is also rung on special occasions such as a wedding or a funeral service. The ringing of the new bell at St. Michael's has ever since its installation created a "joyful noise," reminding all of God's presence in the world. The brass memorial on the left states: "This bell calls the congregation in loving memory of Jane Bowe Cote."

Singing joyfully are, from left to right: Reverend Eleanor Panasevich, Dina Bray, Elize Metzler and Lana Agnew.

Brink Bush, Organist and Choir Master from 2019 to 2021, is seen standing before the church organ. He studied organ at Peabody Institute, the Juilliard School, and the Eastman School of Music. The music program at St. Michael's has long been of the highest caliber. Bush is one of the leading interpreters of German Romantic organ music in the world today and has performed extensively throughout the United States and Europe. He made his German debut at the Berliner Dom and was featured on American Public Media's "Pipedreams" in a program titled Bach, Bush and Middelschulte. His New York debut was heard at Trinity Church Wall Street during the "Virgil Fox Legacy Twenty-fifth Anniversary Concert Weekend."

The Organ was a gift in 1995 in recognition of the Centennial Anniversary by many devoted members and friends of St. Michael's Church. According to Dr. Richard Bunbury, a noted organist and organ historian, "The Andover Organ Company built a strong reputation in mostly restoring and rebuilding nineteenth-century American organs, especially in the New England area. The mechanical action organ at St. Michael's reflects the company's experience with historical instruments and produces sonorities heard in the rich tradition of American organ building, yet with a bit of British influence. It is well suited to organ literature of all periods."

6

Some of the Rectors and Assistant Rectors of St. Michael's Church

He that hath an ear, let him hear what the Spirit saith unto the churches.

Revelations 3:22

St. Michael's, seen in the 1940s, has since 1895 been led by rectors who continued the parish traditions and have contributed to the Christian ministry in Milton. Unfortunately, though we have a chronology of the rectors of the Church since its founding in 1895, not every rector has a photograph, but each person's contribution is vitally important to the church.

Theodore Irving Reese 1895–1907; W. Dewers Roberts 1907–1911; Henry Boyd Edwards 1913–1921; Vincent LeRoy Bennett 1921–1936; Richard Beasley 1937–1940; James F. Madison 1940–1943; Norman Dambach Goehring 1944–1963; Roger Atkinson Walke, Jr. 1963–1976; Thomas Cleveland (Interim)1976; Robert B. Appleyard, Jr. 1976–1992; Robert "Skip" Windsor (Interim) 1992–1994; Samuel Sewell Rodman III 1994–2010; Sarah Connor (Interim) 2010–2012; Hall Kirkham 2012– present.

But ye are a chosen generation, a royal priesthood, an holy nation, a peculiar people; that ye should shew forth the praises of him who hath called you out of darkness into his marvelous light.

1 Peter 2:9

Reverend Theodore Irving Reese (1873–1931) served as Lay Reader and rector from 1895 to 1907. He prepared at St. Paul's School in Concord, New Hampshire and was graduated from Columbia University and the Episcopal Theological School in Cambridge. Reese was ordained deacon by Bishop Ellison Capers in 1897, and as priest in 1898. After ordination, he became rector of St. Michael's Church where "his sermons were like himself; straightforward, natural, intelligent, and spiritual." He served on the Milton School Committee and as a trustee of the Milton Public Library. In 1907 he became rector of Trinity Church in Columbus, Ohio, a post he retained until 1913, after which he was elected Coadjutor Bishop of Southern Ohio, and was consecrated in 1913 as Coadjutor Bishop of Southern Ohio.

Reverend Vincent LeRoy Bennett (1891–1975) served as rector from 1921 to 1936. He was graduated from the University of Pennsylvania and the Union Theological Seminary, and served as a chaplain in World War I with the rank of lieutenant. Before coming to Milton, he served as curate at Grace Church in Manhattan, and from 1942 to 1945 was associate rector of the Episcopal Church of the Ascension at Fifth Avenue and 10th Street, Manhattan; he also served as rector at St. Alban's Church in Syracuse, New York. It was said of him that he was "deeply sincere and greatly gifted in the art of worship; he left a lasting impression on the parish through his sermons and his reading of the services."

Right: Reverend Norman Dambach Goehring (1894–1975) was graduated from Wittenberg College and the Lutheran Seminary. He received his M.A. from Harvard, and Wittenberg conferred upon him the honorary degree of Doctor of Divinity. He served as rector of St. Michael's Church from 1944 to 1963. Previous to entering into the ministry of the Episcopal Church in 1941, he served in 1918 as interim pastor at the Luther Memorial Church in Madison, Wisconsin, then as acting pastor from 1918–1919, and pastor for students from 1919–1920. In the 1940s Reverend Goehring assumed responsibility for Loch Haven in Meredith, New Hampshire and for many summers he operated the Diocesan Conference and Vacation Center there. He served on the Boston City Mission, the Diocesan Refugee Committee and the Clericus Club.

Below: Reverend Roger Atkinson Walke (1914–1996) prepared at Virginia Episcopal School in Alexandria, Virginia, and was graduated from Princeton, magna cum laude. During his career he received an MDiv degree at the Theological Seminary of Virginia. He spent two years farming, then taught at Virginia Episcopal School until WWII. He entered the Army's Ordnance Department as a private and served four years, rising to captain; he was awarded the Army's Commendation Medal. He taught at St. Paul's School in Baltimore, and at Virginia Episcopal School, where he was assistant headmaster. He was headmaster of Porter Academy in Charleston, South Carolina, then headmaster of Virginia Episcopal School in Lynchburg, Virginia, and rector of Christ Church in Blacksburg, Virginia. He was rector at St. Michael's Church from 1963 to 1976. During this time, Rev. Thomas Cleveland served at St. Michael's Church between Roger Walke's leadership and Bob Appleyard's. He taught religion and ethics, and coached football and lacrosse at Milton Academy from 1965 until he retired in 1997. He began his ordained life serving as a missionary in Alaska where he and his wife raised four children. He was a champion of native claims to land and helped to restore Nuchalawoyya, an annual coming together and cultural celebration of regional native peoples along the Yukon River.

Reverend Robert Bracewell Appleyard, Jr. prepared at the Brunswick School and was graduated from Allegheny College. He received his Master of Divinity from the Virginia Theological Seminary in Alexandria. He is the son of the Right Rev. Robert B. Appleyard, Bishop of the Episcopal Diocese of Pittsburgh. He served as assistant rector at the Fox Chapel, and as rector of St. Michael's from 1976 to 1992. He was only twenty-nine when he arrived with his wife, Debby, and their almost one year old son, Ben. His youth actually benefited the many changes that were about to occur both in the larger church and at St. Michael's. A new prayer book, the ordination of women and becoming more inclusive, accepting and diverse as a national church were reflected during his sixteen years with the parish, as the new liturgy welcomed newcomers unfamiliar with the Episcopal Church, women parishioners took leadership roles on the Vestry and elsewhere, and the small, intimate parish family grew into a larger, more outreach-focused community of faith. He later served as rector of St. Barnabas Church in Falmouth, Massachusetts.

Reverend Robert "Skip" Windsor served as interim rector from 1992 to 1994. He said "I started the Sermon Group while I was at St. Michael's and was involved with the beginning of the capital campaign for the new Andover organ." He served as rector of Christ Church, Needham and served parishes in Newton and Weston. He is active on Diocesan committees including the Trustees of Donations, the Boston Episcopal Charitable Society, and the Margaret Coffin Prayer Book Society.

Reverend Samuel Sewall Rodman, III, served as Rector from 1994 to 2010. He was graduated from Bates College and Virginia Theological Seminary, and was ordained to the priesthood in 1988. While he was at St. Michael's, the parish carried out major improvements including the renovation of the Church School building, landscape enhancements, measures to make the buildings fully accessible, and the creation of the Garden of Seasons. Rev. Rodman led trips to the Holy Land and Turkey and to New Orleans after Hurricane *Katrina*. He subsequently served on the staff of the Diocese of Massachusetts. In 2017, he was elected the 12th Bishop of the Episcopal Diocese of North Carolina and was consecrated by his predecessor, Presiding Bishop Michael Bruce Curry. The Rt. Rev. Alan M. Gates, Bishop of Massachusetts, observed on his election, "Here in Massachusetts we well know that Sam has an exceptional combination of gifts—creative imagination, engaging personal interaction, keen organizing skills and the heart of a pastor. He will be a strong and wise shepherd." St. Michael's parishioners often commented on Rev. Rodman's remarkable ability to remember everyone's name.

Reverend Hall Kirkham joined St. Michael's in Milton as its eleventh rector after serving as assistant rector at St. Peter's Episcopal Church in Weston. He is a graduate of the Episcopal Divinity School and received his Master of Divinity in 2008. He currently serves as a member of the Samaritans Council, which helps to support and advise the board of Samaritans, Inc.; as a member of the Cathedral Council of the Cathedral Church of St. Paul; as a member of the Milton Interfaith Clergy Association; and as a member of the Racial Justice Commission of the Episcopal Diocese of Massachusetts. Prior to ordained ministry, he was an investment consultant at Cambridge Associates, LLC, where he worked guiding portfolio asset allocation and investment manager selection for endowed non-profits and high net-worth individuals. Rev. Kirkham is the current rector and he and his wife Marjorie live in the Rectory at St. Michael's with their two children, Victoria and Edmond.

Reverend Victor Kazanjian, seen with his wife Michelle, is a graduate of the Episcopal Divinity School and Harvard University. Prior to St. Michael's he served as seminarian associate and community organizer at St. Ann's Parish in New York City. Rev. Kazanjian served as assistant rector at St. Michael's from 1986 to 1990, after which he became the Director of Program Development at the Episcopal City Mission in Boston. He then served for twenty years as Dean of Religious and Spiritual Life at Wellesley College, where he helped pioneer the field of interfaith religious life programs in higher education. The focus of his ministry was threefold: providing spiritual counseling, administration, liturgical leadership, teaching of social issues, and youth and family ministry; designing and directing youth programs for high school and junior high youth at Milton Academy and Milton public schools; founding and directing the Florence Afterschool Program in Roslindale, Massachusetts. In 2013 he was selected to serve as the Executive Director of the United Religions Initiative, a global grassroots intercultural and interfaith peacebuilding network of more than 1,000 groups comprised of people of different religions, spiritual practices and indigenous traditions. At URI Rev. Kazanjian worked in over 100 countries to build bridges of cooperation between people of all beliefs and cultures, supporting grassroots people around the world in meeting their challenges and building cohesive, connected and peaceful communities.

Reverend Ellis Clifton, Jr. attended Robichaud Senior High School and studied Special Education at Central State University in Ohio. He was graduated from Trinity Episcopal School for Ministry in Ambridge, Pennsylvania. He served as associate rector at St. Michael's from 1998 to 2003. St. Michael's youth attended the National Episcopal Youth Event, the National Acolyte Festival, and the National Union of Black Episcopalian conferences during his tenure. He also served as worship leader for the Epiphany School in Boston. He was celebrant when The Most Reverend Desmond Tutu visited the school. He said "I was made very happy to celebrate the Mass and the Archbishop preached. I still remember how the young people, teachers, parents, board members, and press all hung on to every word when the Archbishop preached that day. This day still ranks in the top 5 events in my ordained life." After leaving St. Michael's, he served St. Mary's in Dorchester, Resurrection in Ecorse, Michigan, and retired in 2020 after serving St. Clement's in Inkster, Michigan. He came out of retirement in 2021 and currently serves as Priest-in-Charge at the Episcopal Church of St. Mary the Virgin on Virgin Gorda, British Virgin Islands. Rev. Clifton serves the wider church as a member of the Office of Black Ministries Council of Advice. He says of his time at St. Michael's, "It was a time of genuine love and growth - unique and distinct from that which I have experienced anywhere else in my ministry. I thank God for my time at St. Michael's and I cherish the lasting relationships that continue".

Reverend Eleanor Panasevich served as associate rector from early 2000 to early 2003. She is seen here with Reverend Samuel Rodman celebrating communion in the Garden of Gethsemane during the 2000 parish trip to Israel. Before coming to St. Michael's, she was a deacon at St. Peter's Church in Weston. Rev. Rodman said of her, "Ellie was a grace-filled presence with great pastoral warmth, combined with a deep and accessible spirituality. Ellie's thoughtful preaching, her prayerful approach to all aspects of parish life and her joyful embrace of the congregation marked a period of growing in faith as a congregation."

Reverend Sherry Osborn holds a Bachelor's in Therapeutic Recreation from Green Mountain College, a Master's degree in Outdoor/ Environmental Education from Boston University, an M.Div. from Yale Divinity School and a Certificate of Anglican Studies from Berkeley Divinity School at Yale. She is a priest and nature educator who loves to playfully and prayerfully share her sense of wonder and curiosity with others. Her professional life, ordained and secular, is woven with a delight of nature, people, song, stories and adventure. She was raised in Vermont and worked as a Nature Educator Consultant. She was raised by a family who played, explored and learned from the great outdoors. Ordained an Episcopal priest in 2003, she served as associate rector at St. Michael's from 2003 to 2006 and as rector at St. Mark's Episcopal Church, Springfield, Vermont from 2006 to 2012. She has just completed two years as interim pastor of St. Paul's, Vergennes, Vermont and is currently contemplating what comes next for employment, which includes the question, "What does the Earth ask of me?"

Reverend Ranjit Koshy Mathews graduated from George Washington University with a Bachelor's in Business Administration, and from Union Theological Seminary with a Master's in Divinity with a focus on Contextual Theology. He was associate rector of St. Luke's Episcopal Church in Long Beach, California, and previously a Lecturer in Theology at the Msalato Theological College of St. John's University in Tanzania as a member of The Episcopal Church's Young Adult Service Corps. He served as assistant rector of St. Michael's from 2006 to 2009. He was the rector of St. James Church in New London, Connecticut and was named a Community Partner by the New London chapter of the NAACP. He also served as Partnership Officer for Africa on the Presiding Bishop's staff of The Episcopal Church and was appointed the secretary of the Social Justice and International Policy Legislative Committee for the House of Deputies, and the Chair of the interim Task Force of Dialogue with South Sudanese Anglicans living in the diaspora. In 2021 he accepted the invitation to serve as the Canon for Mission Advocacy, Racial Justice, and Reconciliation in the Episcopal Church in Connecticut. In this new position he will work with parish and diocesan leadership to make real God's realm of justice, love, and peace, with a focus on our commitment to dismantle racism and white supremacy in our nation and in our church.

Reverend Karen Maleri was ordained priest at St. Paul's Episcopal Church in Concord, New Hampshire. She served as Associate Rector at St. Michael's from 2010 to 2013. She became chaplain at Brooksby Village in Peabody and later helped to establish a volunteer program known as the Compassionate Caregivers Group at Havenwood Heritage Heights in Concord, New Hampshire and has been involved with pastoral counseling in several diverse ministerial settings. She is currently Priest-in-Charge at All Saints Episcopal Church in Wolcott, Connecticut.

Reverend Joyce Caggiano served as associate rector at St. Michael's from August 2013 to June 2015 and served as Interim Rector in the summer of 2022; and more recently as Priest-in-Residence at Emmanuel Episcopal Church in West Roxbury. She has served several parishes in the Boston area including St. Paul's Peabody and St. Paul's Newburyport, and she also served in the Diocese of Michigan as the Director of Social Services and Episcopal Community Services in Detroit. She says: "What excites me most about parish life is the people, the community. Today many of us find our lives are fractured and disconnected. The church is a wonderful place for our children and adults to learn the values of a good society, how to recognize justice, share experiences and learn to care about others. Worship in the church provides a place to be together, to work together to make our world a more just and humane place."

Reverend Jennifer Daly has been the associate deacon at St. Michael's since 1994. She attended Episcopal Divinity School from 1986 to 1990, and it was there she decided she was called to the diaconate, not the priesthood. She understands the diaconal vow to "interpret to the Church the needs, concerns, and hopes of the world" as living at the heart of her call. The major focus of Reverend Daly's work has been the founding of two schools, the Epiphany School in Dorchester, and Bridge Boston Charter School in Roxbury. The students who have passed through those schools have been her spiritual guides.

Reverend Jennifer McCracken joined St. Michael's as a seminarian in 2015, then was hired as associate minister when ordained a deacon in 2018, then as associate rector when ordained a priest in 2019. Later that year she moved to the Cathedral Church of St. Paul to become the head of MANNA (Many Angels Needed Now and Always), a ministry with the homeless community in downtown Boston. MANNA seeks not only to welcome folks across differences of class, wealth, culture, race and mental ability, but also to empower all people to claim their place as essential members of our community. St. Michael's continues to maintain a close relationship to MANNA.

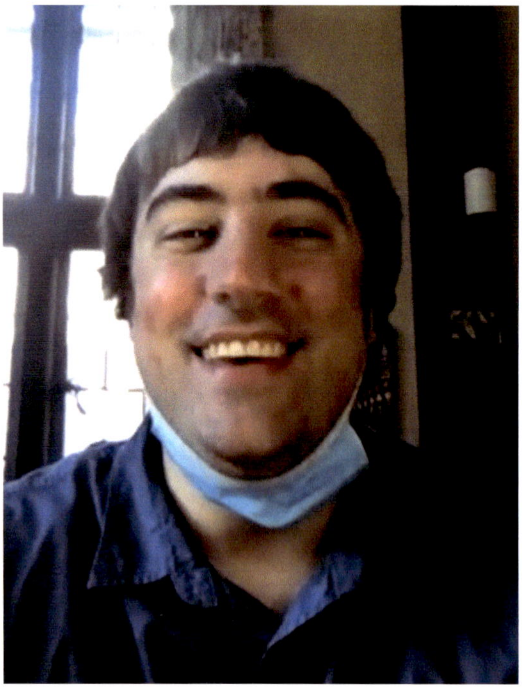

Leo Biocchi joined St. Michael's initially as a Minister to Families, a new initiative begun in January 2020, weeks before the COVID-19 pandemic closed the church building and altered engagement with not just families but all individuals. The Holy Spirit worked its wonders to reveal his considerable skill in streaming and video production, which became his second ministry and carried St. Michael's through the on again/off again rhythm of in-person and virtual gatherings. Today Leo is both Minister of Families and Communications Director.

7

The Women of St. Michael's

Charm is deceitful, and beauty is vain, but a woman who fears the Lord is to be praised.

Proverbs 31:30

A new stained-glass window, given to the Glory of God and in honor of the Women of St. Michael's, was dedicated in 2019. It was said by Joan H. Faulkner to be "Perfect. Visually, spiritually and also inspiring." Seen from left to right are Vicki Rugo, Lana Agnew, Sheila Monks, Reverend Joyce Caggiano, Susan Greendyke Lachevre and Reverend Hall Kirkham at the dedication of the window. The Women of St. Michael's has contributed to the fabric of the church since the St. Michael's Guild started in 1895 with Mrs. Philip Reynolds serving as first President.

Seen here is the First Grade Church School in 1952 with teachers Geraldine Fitch and Marlena Etienne. The church school had grown tremendously since the church was opened in 1895. In 1917 Samuel Lord became the superintendent of the school and he "put heart and soul into the work." During the early years some of the dedicated teachers were Miss Wilde, Miss Luther, Miss Richardson, Miss Ransom and Miss Christie, among many others. Currently the enrollment for the Church School is: Nursery to 4th grade, forty, and 6th to 12th grades, seventeen, with a total of fifty-seven young people.

And all thy children shall be taught of the Lord; and great shall be the peace of thy children.

Isaiah 54:13

Few of us have ever really experienced hunger, but it is prevalent and widespread in our society. St. Michael's often collects and offers food each week in response to the clear imperative of our Lord that we should feed the hungry. It is done each week as a reminder to ourselves and as a symbol in our liturgy that the life and work of the church does not end with Sunday worship. Carol Dildine and a young helper hold a large wicker basket with a sign "Hungry Sunday," asking for contributions of canned food and money that can be donated to the Milton Community Food Pantry and St. Mary's Church in Dorchester.

The Centennial Banner was quilted by Chris Rinderer Kocourek for the 100th Anniversary of St. Michael's in 1995 and hangs in the Parish Hall. Chris recounts that the banner "is an angel holding the dove of peace and standing on earth, although the halo also implies Saint. Top is sky, bottom is ocean, side bars are earth, and the brown surround suggests planting. Books are for knowledge, circles hold the triangles. ... Trinity, triangle at angel's wing top also for Trinity (I probably should have added a flame). Crosses for St. Michael's, the wings are fanciful.....I just liked the color. Can't really remember anything else except I enjoyed making it."

A Window for the Women encouraged the women of St. Michael's to endow a new stained-glass window. As Elizabeth Schmellick said: "This window is so gorgeous, especially with the lovely light and colors of the garden outside. Well done to the artist, stained glass studio, and the committee who oversaw this project and raised funds from so many wonderful people! I love the way the artist framed our view of the outdoors as well as including flora and fauna from around St. Michael's." Here the window is unveiled by Rebecca Domineau, the granddaughter of Bill and Janet Mullen and a descendant of one of the early Women of St. Michael's, to the great joy of the congregation.

Theotokos, the Greek word for "Mother of God," is the theme for the tapestry made by Beth Neville in 1966. It features Mary enthroned on a rectangular Byzantine-style throne, holding the infant Jesus on her lap. She gestures toward Him with her hand, directing our attention to Him as the Divine Child. He holds two symbols of His divinity: the Cross, symbolizing the crucifixion, and the Orb, symbolizing His rule of the divine universe. The Cross is entwined with a serpent, a symbol for healing. They are surrounded by an African mask, symbol for a multi-racial humanity; roses, symbol for Mary; a turtle, symbol for longevity; and butterflies, symbol for beauty. At either upper corner are two Medieval icons, an angel and a skeleton. The red symbols and the blue colors derive from Henri Matisse's late artworks. At the bottom of the tapestry the Greek word for fish, ichthys, appears, and Koine, a Greek word dating to the first century A.D. (Tapestry Gift to St. Michael's Congregation by Elizabeth Neville)

Christ Pantocrator is a tapestry in the Byzantine style made by Beth Neville in 1970. The Greek word describes Christ as "all-powerful," or "powerful creator." Christ's face and figure are derived from Byzantine icons and frescoes in the Cefalù Cathedral in Sicily and the Hagia Sophia mosque/museum/church in Istanbul. The red curving shapes on a blue ground on His robes derive from symbols created by Henri Matisse. Christ raises His hand in the gesture of blessing. His right hand holds His testament. The figure is placed in a mandorla, an almond shape that symbolizes the female womb. The Greek words at the bottom are "Christ" and "Victor". At top left is the medieval symbol for St. John: an eagle; top right, St. Matthew: an angel; lower left, St. Luke: an ox; and lower right, St. Mark: a lion. (Tapestry Gift to St. Michael's Congregation by Elizabeth Neville)

8

The Blessing of the Animals

The righteous care for the needs of their animals, but the kindest acts of the wicked are cruel.

Proverbs 12:10

Reverend Hall Kirkham blesses a dog at the Milton Animal League Shelter. The loving look on this dog's face as he stares up at Rev. Kirkham reinforces the idea that all living creatures, great and small, are loved and give love. The Milton Animal League is a volunteer group dedicated to the rescue, care, and adoption of animals. Nancy Bersani is the Animal Control Officer and with volunteers ensures that the care of animals' housing, food and emotional support are met to the best of their ability.

Lord God, you made Saint Francis of Assisi Christ-like in his poverty and humility.
Help us so to walk in his ways that, with joy and love, we may follow Christ your Son,
and be united to you. Through our Lord Jesus Christ, your Son, who lives and reigns with you and the Holy Spirit, one God, for ever and ever. Amen.

This Blessing of the Animals was held on Sunday, October 9, 2016, in the Garden of Seasons. Reverend Hall Kirkham blessed many loving pets so that they may guard us and guide us for another year. It is said that one day, while St. Francis was travelling with some companions, they happened upon a place in the road where birds filled the trees on either side. He told his companions to "wait for me while I go to preach to my sisters the birds." The birds surrounded him, intrigued by the power of his voice, and not one of them flew away. He is often portrayed with a bird, seen here hovering between his hands.

Ginny, a tabby cat, appears to be the greeter at the Blessing of the Animals, with a brochure and illustration of St. Francis displayed in front of her bed. St. Francis of Assisi, patron saint of animals and of the environment, could be viewed as the original Earth Day advocate. Francis's devotion to God was expressed through his love for all of God's creation. October 4th is the Feast Day of St. Francis.

A large chocolate Labrador Retriever, held by Sargon Donabed, receives a blessing from Reverend Hall Kirkham at the Milton Animal Shelter. In remembrance of St. Francis' love for all sentient beings, guardians sometimes take their animal companions to church for a Blessing of the Animals. August 16th is the annual feast day of St. Roch, the patron saint of dogs. Saint Roch was a noble Frenchman born in 1295. He is recognized as the patron saint of dogs.

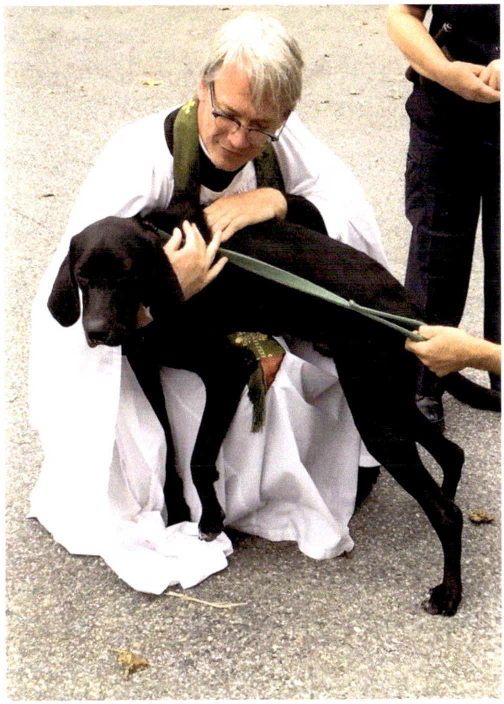

Reverend Hall Kirkham blesses Fred and Missy, the beloved dachshunds of Charlie and Mary Byers Truslow.

> You who created them and called them good:
> bless again these creatures who come to us as a blessing
> fashioned of fur or feather or fin, formed of flesh
> that breathes with your own breath, that you have made
> from sheer delight, that you have given in dazzling variety.

Annually, on or around October 4th, St. Michael's joins Christians around the world in celebrating the Feast of Saint Francis of Assisi with a blessing of the animals. St. Francis, patron saint of animals and the environment, could be viewed as the original Earth Day advocate. He called all animals his "brother" and "sister", and there are stories of him calming a wolf and preaching to the birds. He was canonized in 1228 and remains an icon of kindness and humility to this day. Reverend Sam Rodman, seen here in the center, blesses a child's beloved stuffed monkey.

Seen in the garden in front of the Chapel window, parishioners and friends of all ages gather with their pets and stuffed animals for a blessing. The blessing of animals and pets in the United States has become a mainstream cultural activity, and extends to beloved pets and companions which we depend on or interact with such as service animals. As seen in the photograph, it is a wide spectrum that includes dogs, cats, tropical birds, parrots, canaries, gerbils, goldfish, ferrets, rabbits and mice.

Reverend Hall Kirkham blesses the tiger cat belonging to Sargon Donabed. The 17th of March is the day of St. Gertrude of Nivelles, patron saint of cats; she was a seventh-century abbess who, with her mother Itta, founded the Abbey of Nivelles located in present-day Belgium. Since the Middle Ages, St. Gertrude de Nivelles has been portrayed with rodents and as cats are thought of as the natural predator of rats and mice, it doesn't take much imagination to extend Gertrude's patronage to protecting cats.

> St. Francis - Pray for Our Pets. You blessed us with all living creatures. who are our friends and who bring us so much joy in life. Their presence very often helps us get through trying times.

Even hens receive a blessing! In the foreground is a Barred Plymouth Rock hen and a Silver Laced Wyandotte hen with Sargon and Tiamat Donabed.

> Live without fear: your Creator loves you, made you holy, and has always protected you. Go in peace to follow the good road and may God's blessing be with you always. Amen.

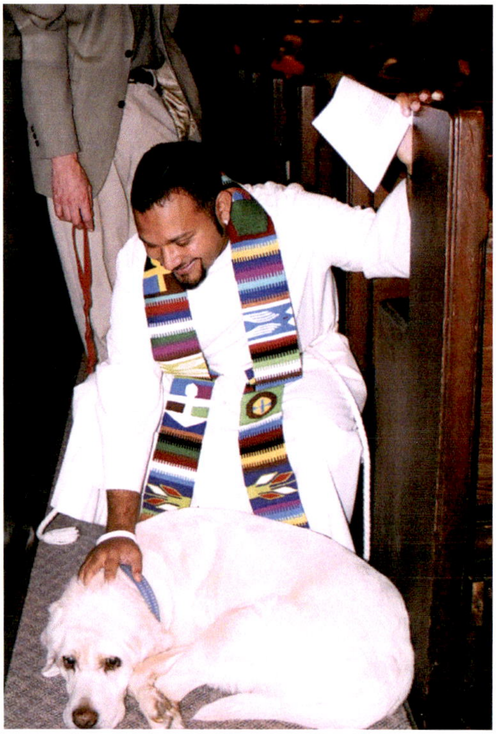

Rev. Ranjit Mathews oversaw the Blessing of the Animals in the church on a rainy day in 2008. Here he blesses a white Labrador Retriever dog that lies down in the side aisle of St. Michael's for the blessing. He lays his hand on the dog, offering a blessing to thank God for the gift of all animals.

And every creature which is in heaven,
and on the earth, and under the earth,
and such as are in the sea, and all that
are in them, heard I saying, Blessing, and
honour, and glory, and power, be unto him
that sitteth upon the throne, and unto the
Lamb for ever and ever.

Revelation 5:13

The Blessing of the Animals service is given in honor of St. Francis, whose love of animals is legendary. Reverend Hall Kirkham stands in front of the altar in the Garden of Seasons as pets and their owners gather around him, each to receive his blessing.

9

Moving Towards the Future

I will instruct thee and teach thee in the way which thou shalt go: I will guide thee with mine eye.

Psalm 32:8

In 1990, the St. Michael's congregation created the Building for the Next Century Campaign, designed to renovate the Church School building, improve the grounds with a landscape design and plantings, and provide handicapped accessibility. Bringing the church into the twenty-first century was one way to become inclusive. As Reverend Hall Kirkham said, "each person has a vital role to play, as we strive to bear witness to God's goodness."

> We believe that every person is a beloved child of God, all of us have gifts to offer, and we each travel our own journey with God. As a community of faith, our mission is to support and foster spiritual growth within our parish family, in the town of Milton, and in the world beyond through worship, education, stewardship, and outreach. We believe in following the teachings of Jesus Christ, whose life, death, and resurrection saved the world.

A drawing of the proposed renovations, additions and changes outlined in the Capital Campaign was submitted to St. Michael's by Catlin & Associates, Architects of Boston. The colored sketch shows St. Michael's Church on the left and the Parish Hall in the center. CBA Landscape Architects Clara Batchelor and Dennis Chagnon transformed the area. As Sheila Monks said, "This courtyard, in all its beauty, is a symbol of that extraordinary sense of community. This is a welcoming and restful place, spacious and intimate at the same time ... the open space echoes with memories of us, calling us to come together again."

Members of the congregation met in the church garden after services not just to enjoy a large sheet cake and punch to celebrate the kickoff of the Capital Campaign, but to also join in a sense of fraternity and hope for the future of St. Michael's as it moved into the twenty-first century.

> One hundred years ago our forefathers here gathered to build this church.
> They poured their wealth as those before them poured their very blood,
> into this place for us, they built for us, and we must build now that our children's
> children may worship freely as we do today.

Kay Herzog

This young parishioner is certainly dressed for the job as a project manager with his yellow plastic construction hat. Seen here is Isabel Ford and her son Teddy Hill, with an ample supply of yellow construction hats for all at the ready!

The Capital Campaign saw the area in front of the Parish Hall reconfigured with a new stone wall, stairs, and plantings of trees and shrubs. Thanks to the Landscape Committee and generous parishioners, the renovations made a significant impact on the church grounds. Ken Conklin said that the project was "the spirit of leadership, the kind of leadership that not only carries us forward but instills within us the excitement and desire to make ourselves better." (Photo by Peter B. Kingman)

As part of the redesigning of the grounds, a stone terrace wall was built and given in 2002 to the Glory of God and in loving memory of Edith Wolcott Devens (1908–1998) by members of her family. Sitting on either side of the bronze marker are William M. Iler and Edith Wolcott Devens Iler. The Terrace Garden in the rear was given in 2003 in memory of Bunty Armstrong by her family.

Now the Lord God planted a garden in the east, in Eden; and there he put the man he had formed, and The Lord God made all kinds of trees grow out of the ground—trees that were pleasing to the eye and good for food.

Genesis 2:8-9

On a glorious summer morning, Reverend Hall Kirkham held a service in the Garden of Seasons, a place of reflection and quiet. Flowering trees, shrubs and large trees allow dappled sunshine to grace the spot.

So then neither is he that planteth anything, neither he that watereth; but God that giveth the increase.

1 Corinthians 3:7

The Altar in the Garden of Seasons was given to the Glory of God and in memory of Eleanor Tileston Eustis Jones (1915–1977). It is made of roughhewn granite in a simple and unadorned traviated design set on stone pavers. Here the altar is prepared for services with a linen altar cloth, brass candlesticks, a Bible in its brass lectern stand and a chalice. It is a simple service held in the peaceful flower and shrub-planted garden.

A cool Easter morning in the Garden of Seasons brought parishioners to this service with a flaming brazier that represents the light of Christ.

> The Lord God took Abram outside and said, "Look up at the sky and count the stars, if you can. Just so," he added, "shall your descendants be." Abram put his faith in the LORD, who credited it to him as an act of righteousness. When the sun had set and it was dark, there appeared a smoking fire pot and a flaming torch, which passed between those pieces. It was on that occasion that the LORD made a covenant with Abram, saying: "To your descendants I give this land, from the Wadi of Egypt to the Great River, the Euphrates."
>
> Genesis 15:5-6, 17-18

The Garden of Seasons accommodates the burial of wooden cremation urns along its low stone walls that curve across the lawn and are marked with slate markers for those interred there. The elements of God's creation are blended to create a space of beauty and serenity, contributing to an environment appealing to families and children, and comforting the bereaved. These children are enjoying an Easter egg hunt, ensuring that the future generation knows those who were once parishioners of St. Michael's Church.

> And God shall wipe away all tears from their eyes; and there shall be no more death, neither sorrow, nor crying, neither shall there be any more pain: for the former things are passed away.
>
> Revelation 21:4

Hill House was named in honor of Kenneth and Marguerite Hill. The cottage was built by Alanson Hall Sturgis, an architect and illustrator who built this as a dower house when he and his wife Mary Wharton Sturgis retired and sold their house on Milton Hill. He prepared at Groton School and was graduated from Harvard, later attending the Harvard Architectural School. He worked as a draftsman in the architectural office of Putnam and Cox and later that of his uncle R. Clipston Sturgis. He later was principal at Sturgis Associates, Inc. There is a plaque to Sturgis in the choir; he served as a member of the choir for thirty-two years. (Photo by Peter B. Kingman)

10

Who We Are

So we, being many, are one body in Christ, and every one members one of another.

Romans 12:5

Members of St. Michael's Church celebrated the 65th Anniversary of the church on All Saints Day in 1960 with a buffet supper served in the Parish Hall. In the center of the photograph is The Reverend Norman Goehring with Mrs. Goehring to the left.

> The Church shall never perish. Her dear Lord to defend, to guide, sustain, and cherish, is with her to the end.
>
> Samuel John Stone

A detail of a larger photograph shows members of St. Michael's at the 50th Anniversary Banquet at the Milton Club in 1945. Standing in the rear is Rev. Norman D. Goehring, third from the left, his wife Emily Boggess Goehring on the left, and his daughter Emily G. Martin and her husband Frank Bucha Martin, Jr. on the right. What is interesting is the wide spectrum of ages from children to adults at the celebration. It was said that "Now in the fiftieth year of St. Michael's history, we look back with deep gratitude and offer a prayer of thanksgiving in our hearts that God gave to that little group who met in 1895 the vision of a church which would further the Kingdom of Heaven on earth."

Seen here are four longtime stalwart members of St. Michael's. From left to right: Loyola Sylvan, Betty Musgrave, Francy Hays and Connie Corson.

The shared time with fellow members, as well as the serving of traditional picnic food and activities for children are an ideal way for members of all ages to get to know each other while having a lot of fun. The Annual Parish Picnic was held after services. Seen from left to right are: Alana Wilson, Anna Wilson, Joan Faulkner, Karen Morrison, Marilyn Cheney, Michael Theobald, Margaret Buttress, Steve Wilson and Jamie McKnight.

A Shrove Tuesday Pancake Supper was followed by a Talent Show held in 2006 in the Parish Hall in honor of one of the mission trips to New Orleans after the disaster wrought by Hurricane *Katrina*. Seen in a lineup with their Mardi Gras beads swinging are, from left to right: John Ahonen, Sheila Monks, Judy Rice and Marilyn Cheney, each with their script at the ready.

St. Michael's Church version of Bess Allen's Pancakes

Ingredients (for 6 cakes):
1 cup flour
1 cup buttermilk (or more, if needed)
1 egg
1 teaspoon baking soda
1 teaspoon salt

Mix until smooth, and ladle into a hot pan and turn when golden.

It's not quite the Vincent Club Drill with these "almost" high kicks, but Dina Roberts Bray patiently coaches top-hatted and bow tied parishioners wearing their red centennial t-shirts who were to perform a skit at the 100th Anniversary celebration at the Milton Hoosic Club. From left to right: Sam Rodman, Carol Young, Ben Phinney, Pam Rodman, Chris Rinderer, and Sue Riley.

Food is an important part of any event, and here a group of people meet in the church kitchen to make Bourbon Balls whose intoxicatingly delicious flavor might help to increase the generous bids at the auction. Holding a bottle of Jim Beam bourbon in one hand and a large bowl of Bourbon Balls in the other is an aproned Joan Faulkner. Her assistants from left to right are: Nancy Graham, Ken Conklin, Adam Sholley, Ted Daiber, Richard Jackmauh, Penny Flanagan, Mollie Stikeleather, and John Duff.

St. Michael's Church Bourbon Balls

Ingredients:

2 tablespoons cocoa
1 ½ cups powdered sugar, divided
¼ cup bourbon
2 tablespoons light corn syrup
2 ½ cups crushed vanilla wafers
1 cup broken pecans

Directions:

Sift together cocoa and 1 cup powdered sugar. Combine and stir in bourbon and corn syrup. Add and mix thoroughly vanilla wafers and pecans. Roll mixture into small balls. Dredge in remaining ½ cup powdered sugar.

The annual Christmas Auction is preceded with a party in the parish hall so the auction items can be seen, admired and bid upon. The silent auction features tables filled with the items, along with sheets for people to place bids. However, for the higher ticket items, there is a live auction, where the bidding is fast and furious! Enjoying the festive atmosphere of the party prior to the auction are, from left to right: Charlie Truslow, Mary Byers Truslow, Leslie James and Robin Putnam.

Sunrise Service on Easter was held at Hutchinson Field on Adams Street in Milton. A group of parishioners gather, facing east, to observe the rising sun. For Christians, the reason for timing a service to coincide with the rising of the sun is important, as it was dawn when the first believers, in every gospel account women, went to the tomb of Jesus and found it empty.

> And, behold, there was a great earthquake: for the angel of the Lord descended from heaven, and came and rolled back the stone from the door, and sat upon it.
>
> Matthew 28:2

The Bishop's Summer Academic & Fun Enrichment program, or B-SAFE, is a ministry of St. Stephen's Youth Programs in the South End, building community with a summer-camp atmosphere that includes hundreds of youth and teens from several Boston neighborhoods across several host sites. The mission is to promote equity in education, employment and opportunity through long-term relationships with young people, their families, and communities. Parishes across the Diocese partner with host sites by choosing a week during the summer camp season to provide lunches, activities, and support, and St. Michael's has partnered for many years with the Church of the Holy Spirit in Mattapan. Seen from left to right are: The Rev. Liz Steinhauser (Director of B-SAFE), Stacy Brown, Allison Norton, Sasha Norton, The Rev. Hall Kirkham, Martha Cotton, Joan Faulkner, John Duff, Janet Larson Mullen, Bill Mullen, and a parishioner from Epiphany West Roxbury.

Members of St. Michael's have long provided a monthly lunch at the Cathedral of St. Paul in Boston as part of the MANNA (Many Angels Needed Now and Always) ministry. This is a ministry with the homeless community in Boston which it seeks not only to welcome people from across differences of class, wealth, culture, race and mental ability, but also to empower all people to claim their place as essential members of the community. This creates an inclusive forum for welcoming people to the lunches through the practices of a welcome, good hearty food and comradery. From left to right are Bill Tennyson, Joan Sholley, Mary Wendell, Dina Roberts Bray, Reverend Hall Kirkham and John Duff.

Members of St. Michael's in Milton went on visits to Milton Abbas, England in 1998 and 2004. The fraternal friendship between the two towns dates back to Reverend Theodore Reese, who had received a fragment on Norman stone from Milton Abbey and had it mounted above the entrance of St. Michael's; the seal of the Town of Milton has a rendition of the Abbey. The street in Milton Abbas is lined with charming thatched roofed houses facing each other. Seen here are those who visited in 1998: Lana Agnew, Edie Clifford, Marilyn Cheney, Ken and Sandy Conklin, Barclay and Barbie Feather, Dina Roberts, Rev. Samuel and Debbie Rodman, Hale and Tucker Smith and their sons Alden and Oliver, Mary and Harry Stubbs, John and Joan Torney and Francy Hays.

After the success of the mission trips to New Orleans, and with the urging of parishioner Susanna Place, St. Michael's began sending groups to support Safe Passage in Guatemala. Each group of about a dozen people was composed of adults, high schoolers and at least one clergy person. Safe Passage is a private, nonprofit Pre-K through 9th grade school which has been in Guatemala City since 1999. Susanna Place serves on the Board of Directors. Their goal is to bring hope, education, and opportunity to the children and families trying to make a living around the city's garbage dump—one of the largest landfills in Central America. Those that went on the trip brought with them much needed school supplies. In Guatemala the group helped in the classrooms, particularly by engaging in conversations and playing educational games with the students to enhance their English proficiency. Our teenagers in particular found the week-long experience life changing. Seen in 2017 are (back): Thomas Hamblet, Lucy Hainline, Duncan Lary, Karen Hainline, Heidi Vaughan, Chuck Zimmerman; (middle): Clara Tennyson, Morgan Smith, Barb Tennyson, William Swanson, Margery Buckingham; (front): Lilly Tennyson, Reverend Hall Kirkham, Cathy Smith.

The highlight of the 2019 Guatemala trip was the creation of a mural for the Women's Center by the young people on the trip. The women asked for a mural and the young folks from St. Michael's sat down with them to ask what they would like on the walls rather than deciding for them. There were many conversations during the trip about what mission really means when time is spent with people suffering like those living in the Guatemala City dump. The painting of the mural was transformative for all who now use the center. Among those on the trip are Richard McCampbell, John McCampbell, Debbie Alsebai, Ayla Alsebai, Jonathan Baum, Samantha Baum, William Swanson, Ruby Hewitt, Foxx Hart and Rev. Jennifer McCracken.

St. Michael's Outreach Commission made a gift of a Jacaranda Tree, *Jacaranda mimosifolia*, to Safe Passage in Guatemala for the school grounds. The school is headed by Thomas Holland and is located in Colonia Landivar, Ciudad de Guatemala. The Jacaranda tree is a favorite of the Guatemalan people because of its fragrant violet-colored blossoms. It provides much needed shade for children while they are playing in the schoolyard. It is said that if a jacaranda flower drops on your head, it means good fortune. The tree represents wisdom, rebirth, wealth and good luck.

The Israel Trip took place in 2000 when a large group of parishioners and friends visited the Holy Land on a tour planned by Heather Putnam. Traditionally, a pilgrimage is a time for healing and reconciliation and can bring a person closer to the experience of Jesus as he approached his death. Christians believe that this will help them to develop spiritually and thereby become closer to God. Among many of the memorable day trips was a swim in the Dead Sea where the salt water made everyone a little more buoyant than usual. (Courtesy Heather Putnam)

During the Israel trip, Rev. Eleanor Panasevich and Rev. Samuel Rodman celebrated communion in the Garden of Gethsemane. The garden, which has many olive trees, is derived from the Aramaic ܓܕܣܡܢܐ meaning 'oil press' and is at the foot of the Mount of Olives in Jerusalem where, according to the four Gospels of the New Testament, Jesus underwent the agony in the garden and was arrested the night before his crucifixion. (Courtesy of Heather Putnam)

After the devastation of Hurricane *Katrina*, volunteers from St. Michael's helped feed individuals and families, rebuild homes and rehabilitate community centers in partnership with Trinity Episcopal Church in New Orleans. Sheila Monks said "God called us to New Orleans to help those in need. It transformed us as well." Seen here from left to right are: Reverend Sam Rodman, John Duff, Deb Rodman, Heather Putnam and Diane Ferrari, among others who volunteered their time and energy to travel to New Orleans. (Courtesy Heather Putnam)

Parishioners of St. Michael's journeyed to New Orleans on several occasions to help in the efforts to assist those affected by Hurricane *Katrina*. The women in the photo are left to right: Lana Agnew, Judy Rice, Cece Lindequist, Sandy Downes and Sheila Monks.

11

The Future of St. Michael's Church

Children's children are the crown of old men; and the glory of children are their fathers.

Proverbs 17:6

A group of boys, sporting their Mardi Gras beads, enjoy the traditional Pancake Supper on Shrove Tuesday, the day before Ash Wednesday when Lent begins. It is a supper of pancakes, sausage, juice, coffee and tea. King Cake, a richly decorated cake with a tiny figure of the Baby Jesus baked into it, an old New Orleans tradition, is also served. The person who finds the Baby Jesus will have happiness and good fortune all year. The name Shrove Tuesday derives from the practice of Christians going to confession the day before Lent, and being 'shriven,' or absolved, of their sins. A bell would be rung to call people to confession, which became known as the "Pancake Bell" and is still rung today. So, the eating of pancakes, be they sweet or savory, is an indulgence in anticipation of forty days of fasting. Clockwise from the boy in the Harvard sweatshirt are: John McCampbell, Deandre O'Donoghue, William Grant, Asher Cardoza, Andrew Millington and Alex Files.

Reverend Jennifer McCracken, holding a fish catch-net with a paper heart in its basket, speaks to the children of St. Michael's who are represented in her sermon on the disciples of Jesus Christ. The Bible speaks of two brothers, Simon and Andrew, who were fishermen casting a net into the Sea of Galilee. As He commenced His preaching ministry, Jesus called them to follow Him and told them that in doing so they were to become "fishers of men." However, in this sermon she encourages the children to fish for hearts!

> And he saith unto them, Follow me, and I will make you fishers of men.
>
> Matthew 4:19

During Family Worship children gather to listen to Reverend Joyce Caggiano preach, assisted by Reverend Hall Kirkham and Deacon Jennifer McCracken. Once a month a service is created especially for families with a concentration on children, the future of the church. Children of all ages assist in the coordination of the service, as well as lead and participate in worship. Sometimes older children will preach sermons, while younger children draw artwork, and all sing to the Glory of God. The free-standing altar was given to the Glory of God and in memory of H. Clifford Turner, Jr. (1931–1966). He was a chief warrant officer and an United States Army aviator who died unexpectedly.

The blessing of school backpacks and book bags is an important part of the annual ritual of returning to school, seen here in September 2021. Grouped around the baptismal font are smiling young children with their newly blessed backpacks, filled with notebooks, pencils, pens, crayons, rulers, scissors, glue sticks and other items used for schoolwork, at the ready!

> Gracious God, we lift to you today, these students. They stand here ready to receive your blessings and they commit themselves to study and learning in the school year ahead. We ask your blessing on each of them. Further, we ask your blessing on these backpacks. They will hold the schoolwork of each student and will be carried from home to school and back again. As these students carry these backpacks, may they be reminded of the love and care of this congregation that surrounds them each school day.

The Boy Scouts of America was inspired by the Boy Scout Association, established by Lord Baden-Powell in Britain, and founded by William Dickson Boyce in the United States in 1910. The Boy Scout slogan is Do a Good Turn Daily. A Boy Scout Troop was begun at St. Michael's in 1914 and led by Scoutmaster Henry Rand Davis (1882–1929) for the next 12 years. It was said of him that he was "Quiet, but firm, he was beloved by all the boys he trained; and the town has reason to be grateful for the many years of his influence." There is a brass memorial plaque to the memory of Henry Davis in the rear of the church. Troop 5 Milton held its Eagle Court of Honor in 2022. Seen in the center is Senator Walter Timilty presenting Senate Citations to, from left to right: Philip Phan, Max Hollingsworth Hays, Max Lenz, and Eliot Hiss.

> The Scout Oath: On my honor I will do my best to do my duty to God and my country and to obey the Scout Law; to help other people at all times; to keep myself physically strong, mentally awake, and morally straight.

A Confirmation Class at St. Michael's proudly poses with Bishop Roy F. Cederholm Jr., Suffragan Bishop of Massachusetts, and Rev. Jennifer Daly. From left to right are Abigail Severance Files, Cecily Lorne Wambold, John Kindelan McCampbell, Eliot West Hiss, Asher Francis Cardoza, John Finnian York, and Kenitra Grace Daly. These young people are making a "mature public affirmation of their faith and commitment to the responsibilities of their baptism and to receive the laying on hands by the bishop." They have now started their journey in life and are sustained in the teachings of the church and truly represent the future of that church.

> I see them, old, young, black and white all gathering on this spot when we are dust.
> The sun shines on them, the church doors open wide.
> The scilla blooms and the Blue Hills abide.
> Link hands! And look, around, above, below
> give thanks for what we own and what we owe.

Kay Herzog

Advent Wreath Making is an important way to create a wreath that celebrates a new liturgical calendar and begins a four-week period of preparation in anticipation of the nativity of Jesus at Christmas. The wreath, which is made of various evergreens, signifies continuous life. The circle of the wreath, which has no beginning or end, symbolizes the eternity of God, the immortality of the soul, and the everlasting life we find in Christ. The first candle, which is purple, symbolizes hope. The second candle, also purple, represents faith. The third candle is pink and symbolizes joy. On the fourth week of Advent, we light the final purple candle to mark the final week of prayer and penance as we wait for the birth of our Savior. On the last Sunday, the white candle in the center is lit. It was even more important in December 2020 when Covid-19 had created a worldwide pandemic and thousands had lost their lives. Allison Norton, Sasha Norton, Veronica Guerrero-Macia, Sargon Donabed, Tiamat Donabed and Noel Marcia-McCampbell continue a tradition that is celebrated not just in church but in the home.

In the Lower Parish Hall children of the church school gathered in November 2021 to make three hundred peanut butter and jelly sandwiches which would be wrapped and brought to the homeless and hungry in the city. The sense of sharing cannot be stressed enough for people of all ages, but these children stepped up to do their part to help alleviate hunger, one sandwich at a time. Seen from the lower left are Reece Rinella, Tiamat Donabed, Aura Sandonato, Brian Rinella, Will Rinella, Charlie Rinella, Enki Donabed. On the far left is Devin Thomas.

This group photograph of parishioners of St. Michael's was taken in 2021 as they gathered in front of the side entrance to the church during the Harvest Gathering. It truly represents what a church family is: people of all ages, all walks of life, all ethnicities, and all races. People who have come together to share in the rich history and traditions of St. Michael's and celebrate not only the 125th Anniversary of the founding of the church in 1895, but also as a group looking to a bright future.

> Look back, look on. Like travelers on a road let us collect ourselves;
> connect ourselves with all who came before us to this place and all who come after.
> We are their heirs; they ours.

Kay Herzog

125 YEARS Celebrating. Caring. Together.

The banner of the 125th Anniversary of St. Michael's is not just to commemorate the anniversary of the founding of St. Michael's Church but is an invitation to join in the celebration of our unity in Christ, while honoring our differences. The rich and ever-evolving history of this very special church has now entered the twenty-first century and invites you to join us in worship, and to become a part of this inclusive and welcoming community.

The mission statement of St. Michael's Church states that "We believe that every person is a beloved child of God, all of us have gifts to offer, and we each travel our own journey with God. As a community of faith, our mission is to support and foster spiritual growth within our parish family, in the town of Milton, and in the world beyond through worship, education, stewardship, and outreach."

Some of the committees and activities that both new members, as well as current members, are encouraged to explore and to serve on are: the Worship Commission, (acolytes, altar guild, flower guild;) Lay Eucharistic Ministers/Lectors/Intercessors; Music Ministry; Sermon Group; Adult Education; Outreach; Bible Study; Milton Food Pantry; Monday Lunch Program; Stewardship Commission; Christmas Auction; Garden of Seasons; Property Committee; Parish Life Commission; Ministry of Caring; Church School.

A Prayer for Guidance

Lord, you have joined us in this community of faith. We thank you for the love and fellowship we share and the many blessings you have given us. Yet we ask that you not let us grow complacent or cling too tightly to what we have. Inspire us to use our resources and talents generously on behalf of others. Fill our hearts with tolerance that we may embrace all people and accept their differing beliefs and opinions. Teach us respect for your earth and compassion for all living things. Help us to raise children who are strong in faith and kind in spirit. In times of danger and uncertainty, protect and comfort us. Strengthen us when we are weak, and forgive us when we fail you. Above all, help us always to keep you in our minds and to love and serve you with our whole hearts. Amen.